Warehouse Theatre Company's

Dick Barton
Episode IV
The Flight of the Phoenix

Book and lyrics by
Duncan Wisbey and Stefan Bednarczyk
with Ted Craig

Dick Barton, Episode IV: The Flight Of The Phoenix
was commissioned by the Warehouse Theatre Company
and the world premiere took place at the Warehouse Theatre,
on Friday 6 December 2002.

Warehouse Theatre Company Regd. Charity No: 272816

warehouse theatre company

Dick Barton
Episode IV
The Flight Of The Phoenix
Book and lyrics by
Duncan Wisbey and Stefan Bednarczyk
with Ted Craig

Dick Barton	Adam Morris
Jock Anderson	Darrell Brockis
BBC Announcer	Kit Benjamin
Snowy White	William Oxborrow
Colonel Gardener	Stephen Aintree
Ladies	Louise Doherty

All other parts are played by members of the company
Music played live by the company

Directed by Ted Craig
Musical Direction Stefan Bednarczyk with Duncan Wisbey
Musical Staging Mitch Sebastian
Designer Ellen Cairns
Lighting Designer James Whiteside
Stage Manager Chris Barham
Assistant Stage Manager Alexandra Nunn
Production Manager Graham Constable
Casting Sooki McShane
National Press Agent KWPR
Dick Barton theatre format Phil Willmott

Adam Morris

Adam trained at Central School Of Speech And Drama. Theatre credits include: Peer Gynt in *Peer Gynt* (University of Chicago); Cannon Throbbing in *Habeus Corpus* (Salisbury Playhouse); Hugh in *Summer Lightening* (Salisbury Playhouse); Jack Worthing *The Importance Of Being Earnest* (Mercury Colchester); *Channel 4 Sitcom Festival* (Assembly Film & TV); Aladdin in *Aladdin* (Ashcroft Theatre, Croydon); Dick in *Dick Whittington* (Bath Theatre Royal); Kenny in *Man Of The Moment* (Mercury Colchester); Marlowe in *She Stoops To Conquer* (Mercury Colchester); Bri in *A Day In The Death Of Joe Egg* (Everyman Cheltenham); Buttons in *Cinderella* (Cambridge Arts and Muffin Prods Basildon); Greg in *Relatively Speaking* (Everyman Cheltenham); Nestor/Oscar *Irma La Douce* (Century Theatre Tour); Cliff in *Cabaret* (Century Theatre Tour); Valentine in *Twelfth Night* (Ludlow Festival); Santo *Ting Tang Mine* (National Theatre); *Fathers And Sons* and *Six Characters In Search Of An Author* (National Theatre); Fowler in *Another Country* (Theatre Royal Northampton); *The Lion The Witch And The Wardrobe* (Westminster Theatre); Aumerle in *Richard II* (Edinburgh Fringe Festival). Television credits include: Mark Devonish in *Doctors* (BBC1); *Black Books* (LWT); *Heartburn Hotel* (BBC); Ed Dudd in *Adam's Family Tree* (Yorkshire Television); Roger in *Babes In The Wood* (LWT); *Back Up* (BBC2 Series); Robin Hood in *Maid Marian And Her Merry Men* (BBC4 Series); *Men Behaving Badly* (Hartswood/BBC); *Growing Rich* (Anglia); *Bergerac* (BBC); *Inspector Morse* (Central). Film includes: Blue Movie Star in *Personal Services* (Zenith).

Darrell Brockis

Darrell trained at Webber Douglas Academy after graduating from St. Andrews University. He is a veteran of all three previous episodes of *Dick Barton* and is delighted to be back at the Warehouse for *The Flight of the Phoenix*. His previous stage roles include: Cassio in *Othello* (Southwark Playhouse); George Hughes in *Equiano*, Herb Maine in *Flow My Tears Said The Policeman* and Mick in *The Focus Group* (all Oval House – Fifth Column

Theatre); Jim O'Connor in *The Glass Menagerie* (BAC and UK tour); Romeo in *Romeo and Juliet* and Lucentio in *The Taming of the Shrew* (RJ Williamson Prods – UK Tour); *Crash* (Warehouse Croydon); Hal in *Henry IV Pts I and II* (Fifth Column) Ferdinand in *The Duchess of Malfi* and D'Anceny in *Les Liasons Dangereuse* (Byre). Most recently he performed in a mummers play for *The Lion's Part* and *The Real Hans Sachs* (Linbury Studio – Royal Opera House). Darrell has also made several short films and work extensively for Live TV.

Kit Benjamin

Kit originally thought he was going to be a musician and, from his late teens onwards, was a conductor of a number of choirs and orchestras. At some point he changed his mind and, while he still maintains a number of musical interests, particularly in violin and singing, he has played a strange variety of characters on stage, both in musical and 'straight' theatre, from the psychopathic Sergeant in Kafka's *In The Prison Colony* to the androgynous role of Mary Sunshine in Century Theatre's national tour of *Chicago*. He toured for the same company in a rare revival of Noel Coward's *Bitter-sweet*. Kit has also performed and recorded the title role in a new musical entitled *Isambard Kingdom Brunel*. Kit's most recent West End performances include *Cats* (New London Theatre) and *Buddy* (Strand Theatre). He also spent a delightful two years playing Pat Levin, a role which he created, in Paul Elliott's production of *Jolson* (Victoria Palace Theatre), on tour in the UK and at The Alexandra Theatre, Toronto. This is Kit's third appearance in the *Dick Barton* canon, having appeared in *Dick Barton I* at Nottingham and *Dick Barton III* last year at the Warehouse.

William Oxborrow

William trained at LAMDA. Theatre credits include: Benvolio in *Romeo And Juliet* (Northcott, Exeter); Fedotik in *Three Sisters* (Southampton & tour); William Featherstone in *How The Other Half Loves* (Palace Theatre, Watford); Horatio in *Hamlet* (Northcott, Exeter); Macready in *Strangers On A Train* (Colchester/Tour); BBC Announcer in *Dick*

Barton – Special Agent (Warehouse Theatre/Tour); Robert in *Boyband* (Gielgud Theatre); Philip in *The Deep Blue Sea* (Royal Exchange, Manchester) directed by Marianne Elliott; Tom in *Hard Times* (Tour for the Good Company); Duncey Cass in *Silas Marner* (Theatr Clwyd); Adam in *Someone To Watch Over Me* (Globe Theatre Group, Warsaw); Dorian Gray in *The Picture Of Dorian Gray* (Gate Theatre, Dublin); Trueman in *The Clandestine Marriage* (Queen's Theatre, Algernon) in *The Importance Of Being Earnest* (Derby Playhouse); Fortnum in *The Madness Of George III* (National Theatre) directed by Nicholas Hytner; Sergeant Ferraby in *The Case Of The Frightened Lady* (Palace Theatre, Watford) directed by Frith Banbury; Rosie in *The Mirror Of The Moon* (Edinburgh Festival) directed by Jonathan Church; Jason in *Over A Barrel* (Palace Theatre), Watford directed by Michael Attenborough; Orpheus in *Eurydice* (Chichester Festival) directed by Michael Rudman; Billy Boy Droog in *A Clockwork Orange* (RSC) directed by Ron Daniels; The Servant in *The Silent Woman* (RSC) directed Danny Boyle; Balthasar in *Romeo And Juliet* (RSC) directed by Terry Hands; Francisco in *Hamlet* (RSC) directed by Ron Daniels. Television credits include: Everard Mountjoy in *The Mrs Bradley Mysteries* (BBC TV) directed by Audrey Cooke; Machiavelli in *The Anarchists* (AGM Aspire Productions); Edward Kynaston in *All The King's Ladies* (Channel 4).

Stephen Aintree

After realising that Liverpool F.C. were never going to offer him the left back/captain job he so earnestly desired, Stephen escaped the civil service, did a degree course and trained at Mountview Theatre School. Theatre work includes: the Clearlake M.C. in *Buddy* (West End and tour); a cheery Bullfrog in *The Ugly Duckling* (Watermill Newbury); Beadle Bamford in *Sweeney Todd* (Holland Park Theatre); and Zangara in *Assassins* (Brighton Komedia). Stephen worked with Lionel Bart playing Clopin the Beggar King in a workshop presentation of Lionel's musical *Quasimodo*, created the role of Dick Rogers in the Bob Carlton musical *Face*, understudied and played Alfred Doolittle in *My Fair*

Lady (Sheffield Crucible) and has appeared in *Happy End* and *The Threepenny Opera* (Theatr Clwyd). In 2002 he was the Abbot and the Duke de Haberdasheri in the national tour of Terry Pratchett's *Truckers*, played 10 different people in Hound Of The Baskervilles (Coventry Belgrade) and has appeared in his first Radio 4 play, *Till The Words Come Back*. Stephen played Scouse in two series of *Heartburn Hotel*, and other television work includes *The Bill, Where The Heart Is, Preston Front, Monarch Of The Glen, 2 Point 4 Children* and Whispering Walter in *The Detectives*. He recently completed his first lead in a feature film, playing Colin in *Dead Money* (Iron Pictures). Stephen is married to actress and award-winning writer Lynn Robertson Hay. Both are committed Christians and live in North London. His big ambition is still to be The Doctor in *Doctor Who*, but he thinks it more likely he will be offered Dalek roles.

Louise Doherty

Louise studied drama at London University (Royal Holloway and Bedford College) and after that trained at the Drama Studio London where she graduated with distinction. Whilst there, she was a runner up in the Carleton Hobbs BBC Radio competition. Selected theatre credits include: one year with the Wigan Pier Theatre Company, Alice in *Alice In Wonderland* (Wimbledon Studio Theatre); Lady Macbeth / Hero in *Macbeth / Much Ado About Nothing* (Rainbow Outside Theatre in West Sussex); Wendla in *Spring Awakening* (Jermyn Street / Tristan Bates Theatre); Hermia in *A Midsummer Night's Dream* (tour of Northern Italy and the Scottish Highlands); Olivier in *Twelfth Night* (Jerash Festival); Prince Arthur in *Life And Death Of King John* (OSC, at the Globe Theatre).

Duncan Wisbey – Author and Musical Director

Duncan has been involved with *Dick Barton* since its first show in 1998 acting in all three episodes, having played Lady Laxington, Sir Stanley Fritters and others in *Episode I*, Swanker of Arabia in *Episode II*, and Juan El Bigglesworth in *Episode III*. Other writing credits include *Jubilation!* (Henley Festival 2002), *Happy and Glorious* (Tour), *Gogo, The Boy with Magic Feet* (winner of three awards at Edinburgh Festival) and three series of Alistair McGowan's *Big Impression*.

Stefan Bednarczyk – Author and Musical Director

Theatre credits as an actor include: *Semi-monde* (Lyric Theatre, Shaftesbury Avenue); *Dick Barton – Special Agent* (Warehouse Theatre, Croydon, and national tour); *Whenever* (Stephen Joseph Theatre); *Jermyn Street Revue* (Jermyn Street Theatre); *5'o'clock* (Edinburgh, Hampstead, King's Head Theatres); *Laughter On The 23rd Floor* (Queen's Theatre, London and national tour); *Schippel The Plumber* (Greenwich); *The La Plays* (Almeida); *The Game Of Love And Chance* (Royal National Theatre); *Sugar Hill Blues* (Warehouse, Hampstead); *Playing Sinatra* (Warehouse, Greenwich); *A Midsummer Night's Dream* (Leicester); *A Midsummer Night's Dream* and *Twelfth Night* (Regent's Park); *Mozart And Salieri* (ATC); *Merrily We Roll Along* and *Noel And Gertie* (Cardiff); *Robert And Elizabeth* (Chichester). Musical direction has included shows at Chichester, Cardiff, Swansea, Leeds, Sheffield, Oxford, Regent's Park, Open Air, Buxton Opera House, Holders Opera Festival (Barbados), Warehouse Theatre, Croydon. Television credits include: *Crocodile Shoes, Crown Prosecutor, EastEnders, Love Hurts, Paul Merton – The Series, Harry Enfield And Chums, Stefan's Guide To Culture, The Grand Style Of Jazz*. Solo cabaret performances include: seasons in London (Pizza on the Park, King's Head Theatre, Jermyn Street Theatre) throughout the UK and abroad in Cannes, Antibes, Monaco, Cologne, New York, Los Angeles, San Francisco, Barbados and Vienna. Film credits include: *Topsy-Turvy*, *Composed* and *Sea Change*. Stefan has been the Musical Director of *Dick Barton – Special Agent* since the first production and is very grateful to the casts – past and present – for their contributions to the musical arrangements.

Ted Craig – Director

Ted is the Artistic Director and Chief Executive of the Warehouse Theatre Company. He commissioned the Dick Barton series and has directed each one of the episodes. Ted's career has included the directorship of the Drama Theatre of the Sydney Opera House and many freelance productions both here and abroad. These include the Off-Broadway productions of *Look Back In Anger* with Malcolm McDowell (Roundabout Theatre); *The Astronomer's Garden* by Kevin Hood (Warehouse and Royal Court Theatre); *Playing Sinatra* by Bernard Kops (Warehouse and Hampstead Theatre); Shakespeare's *The Tempest*, Congreve's *Love For Love*, Moliere's *The Misanthrope* and Feydeau's *The Lady From Maxim's* (Sydney Opera House); *Tarantara! Tarantara!* by Ian Taylor (Theatre Royal, Sydney and Australian tour); *The Elephant Man* by Bernard Pomerance (Melbourne Theatre Company) and Arthur Miller's *The Last Yankee* and Joe Orton's *Entertaining Mr Sloane* (Theatro Ena, Cyprus). His most recent productions are *Blood Royal* by Charles Thomas at the King's Head Theatre and Richard Vincent's *Skin Deep* at the Warehouse Theatre. He co-founded the International Playwriting Festival and is proud of its considerable achievements in discovering and promoting new playwrights over the past seventeen years.

Mitch Sebastian – Musical Staging

Mitch's work has received critical acclaim, particularly for the innovative way he has staged new productions of Broadway Shows: *pippin.co.uk* (directorial debut) (Bridewell Theatre); *Romance Romance* (Gielgud Theatre); *Lucky Stiff* (Bridewell Theatre); *Merrily We Roll Along* (Royal Academy of Music). He is often associated with new works, collaborating with writers on original productions: *Watermark* (Crucible Theatre); *Eyam* (Bridewell Theatre); *Tales My Lover Told Me* (King's Head Theatre); *Hell Can Be Heaven* (Pleasance Theatre); *Twist Off Fate* and *Sing To The Dawn* (both for the Singapore Repertory Theatre). This creative drive has also led to Mitch being involved in many workshops in London and New York. He previously created staging for the Peter Hall Company's *Playhouse Creatures* (Old Vic Theatre); choreographed and staged the world premiere of *La Cava* (Victoria Palace, Piccadilly Theatre) and the national tour of *Iolanthe* (D'Oyly Carte Opera Company). He was commissioned to stage a new oratorio *On The Eighth Day*, by the London Philharmonic Orchestra and subsequently has staged several large-scale productions on their behalf. Mitch has directed and staged many gala concert performances all over the world, ranging from the hugely popular *Magic Of The Musicals* (London Palladium, European and national tours) to intimate cabarets such as *It Takes Two* (Jermyn Street Theatre) and *Three Lost Souls* (BAC and King's Head Theatre). He also staged Ria Jones' television special *For One Night Only* (BBC Wales) and Marti Webb's 1994 *Gershwin Concert Tour*. More recently he directed the Launch of Singapore's new television channel TV Works. After completing the music of *Sammy Davis Jr, Dean Martin and Frank Sinatra* is due to open in the West End.

Ellen Cairns – Designer

Ellen Cairns trained at Glasgow School of Art and The Slade. Her last collaboration with Ted Craig at the Warehouse Theatre was *Happy And Glorious* in 1999. She designs extensively in this country and abroad. Recent credits include: the current 25th anniversary production of *Educating Rita* (Liverpool Playhouse) updated by Willy Russel; *Les Miserables* and *Miss Saigon* in Estonia; Arthur Koestler's *Darkness At Noon* (Stockholm Stadsteater). She is currently working on *Moon On A Rainbow Shawl* for Nottingham Playhouse, *Bent* for Tallinn, *West Side Story* and a further production of *Miss Saigon* for Helsinki.

James Whiteside – Lighting Designer

James Whiteside graduated from The University of Birmingham in 1999. For the Warehouse he has lit *Dick Barton Episode III* and *Skin Deep* as well as *Blood Royal* at the King's Head, all directed by Ted Craig. Other recent credits include *The Coffee Lover's Guide To America* and *The Singing Group* (Chelsea Theatre). For Tall Stories Theatre Company work includes *The Gruffalo* on a national tour and *Snow White* at the Barbican Pit, which will play at the New Victory, Off Broadway in the New Year. Work in opera and musicals includes: the current national tour of *Calamity Jane* with Toyah Willcox; *La Traviata* (Surrey Opera) and *Matins For The Virgin Of Guadalupe II* (BAC). James also assisted Hugh Vanstone on the recent national tour of *Godspell* and will be lighting a new US Tour of *Madame Butterfly* for London City Opera next year.

Chris Barham – Stage Manager

Chris trained on the Stage Management and Technical Theatre course at RADA. His interests in Entertainment and namely Theatre were paramount before training, having lit, provided sound and set for many musical productions and fashion shows. This interest in everything technical sprung from setting up his own mobile discotheque business at only eight years old. Credits whilst at RADA include: *Napoli Milionaria* (Deputy Stage Manager); *A Small Family Business* (Stage Manager); and *Devil In Drag* (Sound Designer) This is Chris's first engagement since graduating from RADA in July 2002.

Alexandra Nunn – Assistant Stage Manager

Since graduating from the Courtyard Theatre Company, Alex has been involved in numerous productions in roles ranging from AM to Lighting Designer. Credits include: DSM/Operator *Sweeney Todd* (Bridewell Theatre); Touring Stage Manager *Envision* (The Moving World Theatre); ASM *Skin Deep* (Warehouse Theatre); Stage Manager *Big Boys* (Warehouse Theatre); Technical Manager (Etcetera Theatre, Camden).

Graham Constable – Production Manager

Graham studied Stage Design and Performance at the Rijksakademie, Amsterdam, and under Josef Szajkna at the Studio Theatre, Warsaw. He returned to London and formed ARC, a mixed media performance group. Graham has constructed settings and properties for film, television and theatre, for companies as diverse as BBC TV, Venezuelan TV, the Edinburgh Wax Museum and Glydebourne Opera. As the Warehouse Theatre's Production Manager, he has built over forty shows.

This year the Warehouse Theatre celebrates its 25th Anniversary. Founded in 1977 in one of Croydon's few remaining Victorian industrial buildings it soon built a national reputation for producing and presenting the best in new writing. In 1986 it launched the prestigious International Playwriting Festival. Having inaugurated a partnership with the leading Italian playwriting festival, the Premio Candoni-Arta Terme, in 1995, selected plays are now seen in Italy offering the potential for further performance opportunities in Europe. A new Greek partnership has now been created with Theatro Ena in Cyprus. Previous winners such as Kevin Hood, whose play *Beached* won the first ever Festival, have gone on to achieve incredible success nationally and internationally. Kevin's two subsequent plays for the Warehouse, *The Astronomer's Garden* and *Sugar Hill Blues,* both transferred, the first to the Royal Court and the second to Hampstead Theatre. His most recent work includes the BBC2 series *In A Land Of Plenty.*

Today the Warehouse Theatre is acknowledged as one of the foremost theatres for new playwriting in the country. Other hugely successful productions have included *Sweet Phoebe,* by Australian playwright Michael Gow, which saw the London stage debut of Cate Blanchett, *Iona Rain* (winner of the 1995 International Playwriting Festival) and *The Blue Garden,* both by acclaimed playwright Peter Moffat and critically acclaimed *The Dove* by Bulgarian playwright Roumen Shomov. A continuing success is the company's stage version of *Dick Barton Special Agent.* First produced at the Warehouse in December 1998 it was an instant success, was brought back by popular demand in 1999 and then toured nationally. More success then followed with Episodes II and III.

The theatre is also proud of its partnership with other companies who share the commitment to new work, discovering and promoting the fledgling Frantic Assembly and other companies like Red Shift, Theatre Alibi, Look Out Theatre and Hijinks. Long standing partnerships with Black Theatre Co-op (now Nitro) and Tara Arts has been in the forefront of the theatre's commitment to access and equality. It has a thriving youth group, a busy programme of multi-cultural work for young people and a Writers Workshop programme.

Warehouse Theatre

Artistic Director	Ted Craig
Administrative Director	Evita Bier
Marketing Manager	Damien Hewitt
Assistant Administrator	Jenny Harrington
Education Co-ordinator	Rose Marie Vernon
Box Office Manager	Emily Collison
Production Manager	Graham Constable

Board of Management
Brenda Kirby (chair), Cllr Eddy Arram, Celia Bannerman, John Clarke, Tim Godfrey, Dr Jean Gooding, Mike Hodges, Malti Patel, Michael Rose, Mia Soteriou, Cllr Martin Tiedmann, Cllr Mary Walker

Patrons
Lord Attenborough CBE, George Baker, Lord Bowness CBE DL, John Gale OBE, Joan Plowright CBE, Robert Stiby JP

Funding Bodies
London Borough of Croydon
Association of London Government

Sponsorship
Warehouse Theatre Company are grateful for ongoing sponsorship from HSBC, The Peggy Ramsay Foundation and Croydon Advertiser Group.

The
Peggy
Ramsay
Foundation

The Warehouse Theatre Company's International Playwrighting Festival
A National and International Stage for New Writing

The International Playwriting Festival 2002 celebrated seventeen years of discovering, nurturing and promoting the work of new playwrights, consolidating the role of the Warehouse Theatre Company as a powerhouse of new writing.

Plays are also presented in Italy at the leading Italian playwriting festival Premio Candoni-Arta Terme. Many selected plays also go on to production in Britain and abroad. IPF 2002 marked a seven year partnership with Premio Candoni-Arta Terme and a three year partnership with Theatro Ena Nicosia.

The Festival is held in two parts. The first part is a competition with plays entered from all over the world and judged by a panel of distiguished theatre practitioners. The second is a presentation of the best selected work from the competition, which takes place every November. Entries for IPF 2003 will be received from January 2003.

Recent Successes

The Shagaround, the debut play by Southampton based playwright Maggie Nevill, was selected from the festival in 1999. The play was then showcased in Italian at the Premio Candoni-Arta Terme and at the Tricycle Theatre in English. The play, produced by the Warehouse Theatre Company and the Nuffield Theatre, Southampton has since toured at Nuffield Theatre (Southampton), Ashcroft Theatre (London), Soho Theatre (London) and Brighton Theatre Royal.

The Dove by Bulgarian playwright Roumen Shomov, selected in 1999, was produced at the Warehouse Theatre in April-May 2000, was showcased at the Premio Candon Arta Terme the same year, and went on to be produced twice in Bulgaria.

"This fascinating play by Roumen Shomov...an accurate reflection of the lunacy of daily life" *The Guardian*.

Real Estate by Richard Vincent, selected in 1994, was produced in Italy by Il Centro per la Drammaturgia Contemporanea "H" and Beat 72 at Teatro Colosseo in Rome December 2001. Richard has now received a commission from Film Council.

51 Peg by Phillip Edwards, the 1998 Festival selection, was showcased at the Premio Candoni Arta-Terme in Italy (May 1999) and was produced at the Edinburgh Festival 2000.

"Edwards' script is exceptional...goes beyond the norm that most playwrights would find comfortable" *Edinburgh Evening News*

The Ressurectionists by Dominic McHale, the 1997 Festival selection, was premiered at the Warehouse Theatre in 1998, as a co-production between the Warehouse Theatre Company and the Octagon Theatre, Bolton. It was also performed at the Octagon the same year.

"Dominic McHale's entertaining debut...hilarious" *Evening Standard*

Just Sitting by Andrew Shakeshaft
Premiere at Premio Candoni Arta-Terme 2001.

Knock Down Ginger by Mark Norfolk
Premiere at Premio Candoni Arta-Terme 2002.

The selected plays for the International Playwriting Festival 2002 were *Paradiso* by Raymond Ramcharitar, *Black Other* by Dystin Johnson, *Blue Day* by Riou Benson, *A Scent of Lilac* by Lindy Newns and *Destroy Jim Hasselhoff* by Amy Jump.

The Shagaround

The Dove

Sweet Phoebe

First published in 2002 by Oberon Books Ltd.
(incorporating Absolute Classics)
521 Caledonian Road, London N7 9RH
Tel: 020 7607 3637 / Fax: 020 7607 3629

e-mail: oberon.books@btinternet.com
www.oberonbooks.com

A catalogue record for this book is available from the British
Library.

ISBN: 1 84002 356 2

Cover illustration: Peter Holt

Printed in Great Britain by Antony Rowe Ltd, Chippenham.

Characters

COLONEL GARDENER
CLEMENT ATLEE
LORD REITH
DICK BARTON
PRISON GUARD
BBC ANNOUNCER
JOCK ANDERSON
SNOWY WHITE
MRS HORROCKS
CHARLES
BARMAID
PETER, the Professor
MR HUGE
LAUGHING JAKE
LATE BOB
THE ANGEL
TAPPY
POTTY
BAZ
MACKY
NATHANIAL
JEDAKAIAH
GYPSY
VERA
DENNIS
GORKY
NURSE
KENNY
THE KING

Musical Numbers

handwritten: 1947 with 20ᵗʰ century awards

Act One

THE DESCENT TO HELL
Music: 'Don Giovanni' by Mozart – Dick Barton, Guard

DORABELLA
Music: 'Carmen Flower Song' by Bizet – Dick Barton

WICKED WAYS
Music: 'Gendarme Song' by Offenbach – Huge, Bob, Peter, Jake, Dick Barton, Charles

BARTON'S PRAYER
Music: 'Musetta's Waltz Song' by Puccini – Dick Barton

ANGEL VISION SEQUENCE
A: Music: 'Love is like a Red, Red, Rose' – Jock
B: Music: 'The Devil's Gallop' – Snowy
C: Music: 'Ruler of the Queen's Navee' by Sullivan – Colonel Gardener

Act Two

GOODBYE CHARLIE
Music: 'Goodbye Dolly Grey and Tipperaree' – Dick Barton, Charles, Macky, Tappy, Potty, Baz

FORTUNE TELLER SONG
Music: 'Hungarian Dance No.5' by Brahms – Gypsy, Dick Barton

VENDETTA SONG
Music: 'Dies Irae' by Mozart – Huge

THE SIDEKICK SONG
Music: 'Funiculi, Funicula' by Denza – Snowy, Gorky, Dick Barton

THE SIDEKICK SONG (reprise)
Music: 'Funiculi, Funicula' by Denza – Jock, Snowy, Dick Barton, Kenny

Rules of Conduct

1. Barton is intelligent as well as hard-hitting. He relies as much upon brains as upon brawn.

2. He only uses force when normal, peaceful means of reaching a legitimate goal have failed.

3. Barton never commits an offence in the criminal code, no matter how desirable the means may be argued to justify the end.

4. In reasonable circumstance, he may deceive but he never lies.

5. Barton's violence is restricted to clean socks on the jaw. When involved in a brawl which results in victory for the Barton side, he must be equally matched or out-numbered.

6. Barton's enemies have more latitude in their behaviour but they may not indulge in actually giving any injury or punishment which is basically sadistic.

7. Barton and his friends do not wittingly involve innocent members of the public in situations which would cause them to be distressed. For example, a motor car cannot be requisitioned for the purpose of chasing bandits without the owner's permission.

8. Barton has now given up drink altogether. No reference should be made to its existence in the Barton circle. The villains may drink but never to excess. Drunken scenes are barred.

9. Sex, in the active sense, plays no part in the Barton adventures. This provision does not of course rule out the possibility of a decent marriage (not involving Dick personally) taking place.

10. Horrific effects in general must be closely watched. Supernatural or pseudo-supernatural sequences are to be avoided – ghosts, night-prowling, gorillas, vampires.

11. Swearing and bad language generally may not be used by any character. This ban ranges from 'bloody' through 'God', 'Damn' and 'hell' to ugly expressional currently heard in certain conversations.

12. Political themes are unpopular as well as being occasionally embarrassing.

BBC Memo, 27 August 1947

ACT ONE

Scene 1

COLONEL GARDENER's office.

COLONEL GARDENER is at his desk. To one side of him is LORD REITH, chairman of the BBC. To the other side is CLEMENT ATLEE, the Prime Minister. Before them, cowed, stands DICK BARTON.

COLONEL GARDENER: Gentlemen, I think it is time to bring this court martial to a close. Dick Barton, Special Agent, in the presence of myself, Colonel Reginald Gardner of MI5, the Prime Minister Mr Clement Atlee and Lord Reith, Director General of the BBC, you have been found guilty of 'conduct prejudicial to good order and military discipline'. The three counts on which you have been found guilty are as follows. A. You lost your cool. A special agent never loses his cool. B. You employed a profanity prohibited by the BBC guidelines. I draw your attention to Section Eleven of the Rules Of Conduct: *Swearing and bad language generally may not be used by any character. This ban ranges from…* – well I can't say that…*through…* – can't say that either…or that, or that – *…to ugly expressions currently heard in certain conversations.* C. You allowed your upper lip to become unstiffened. This is not British and, I need not remind you, it is very far from cricket. Therefore, as your superior, it falls upon me to discharge you from your duties as Britain's top special agent. I must ask you to hand over your gun, your hat and your mackintosh. I have nothing further to add. Mr Prime Minister.

CLEMENT ATLEE: Thank you Colonel Gardener. Mr Barton. This is indeed a most regretful day. I never trusted you myself, Barton, and it is no surprise to me that I must now, on behalf of Her Majesty's Government, strip you of your national hero status. From now on, subjects will no longer speak your name. You have abused the trust and loyalty of the British listening public. People looked up to you, Barton. They hung on your every word. Children raced home from school in time to hear your adventures. Families gathered around their wireless sets, anxious to hear the strains of your nightly movements. You were a national institution. You represented hope and stability in an insecure time. Britannia weeps today. The British government must be seen to be taking a tough line on upper labial flaccidity. We must not be seen to be a soft touch and as a consequence not only are you no longer to be a national hero, but in order to protect the integrity of this nation, you are to be declared public enemy number one. I have nothing more to say. Good day.

COLONEL GARDENER: Well I think that just about wraps everything up…

CLEMENT ATLEE: Oh. One more thing. You are to go to prison for the rest of your natural life.

DICK BARTON: What?

CLEMENT ATLEE: I said good day Mr Barton.

DICK BARTON: But…this is ridiculous. I've been framed. Don't I at least get a fair trial?

CLEMENT ATLEE: What do you think this is?

DICK BARTON: But where's my defence?

CLEMENT ATLEE: You haven't got one. You're guilty. That's the whole point.

DICK BARTON: No I'm not! Lord Reith, as Chairman of the BBC, surely you –

LORD REITH: Mr Barton! May I remind you that it has been announced on the BBC that you are guilty. Therefore you are guilty.

DICK BARTON: But I'm not!

LORD REITH: Do you dare to suggest that the BBC would give false information? You should know by now that once something has been announced on the BBC it is as good as gospel. No matter how innocent you may think you are, nation has spoken peace unto nation for longer than you've been a special agent, and nobody would take the word of an individual over the might of the corporation. Take your punishment like a man.

COLONEL GARDENER: It's for your own good, Barton, and the good of the nation. Have you anything to say?

DICK BARTON: Yes actually. I have. What's to happen to my programme?

LORD REITH: It was decided at three by the powers that be at the BBC, that is to say me, that your programme shall continue to be broadcast every evening at its usual time, until it reaches its natural conclusion.

DICK BARTON: Natural conclusion? But what will that be? Am I to leap to safety, clear my name and win the day or…no…surely you're not going to…? What's to happen to me?

LORD REITH: That, Barton, is up to God, the Scriptwriters…and you.

Lighting on BARTON as he looks 'to camera'.

BBC ANNOUNCER: This is the BBC broadcasting from London. It's 6:45 and time for the final exciting instalment of…Dick Barton, Special Agent.

Music: 'The Devil's Gallop'.

And so the dreaded fateful day comes when our hero falls to his doom. A day that we all secretly feared would come. A day that was prophesied in the Revelations section of the BBC Handbook. We must all be str–… I'm sorry… (*He gets out a hanky.*) We must all be strong, put on a brave face. Smile through the tears. Make your Mum a nice cup of Earl Grey, there's a good lad, two sugars. Slip yer girl a fiver, tell her to go up West and get herself something nice. But spare a thought for the nation's hero as he prepares for his first day under lock and key in the none-too-salubrious surroundings of Dartmoor Prison.

Scene 2

The Descent to Hell

GUARD: (*Sings.*)

MR BARTON – THE PRIS'N IS WAITING
ALL OF DARTMOOR IS CELEBRATING
OVER HALF THE PEOPLE IN HERE
ARE IN HERE BECAUSE OF YOU:
JUST IMAGINE HOW THEY'RE FEELING –
A REUNION'S OVERDUE!

DICK BARTON: (*Sings.*)

IT'S A DREAM, IT'S A DREAM
I'LL WAKE UP AND FIND I'M DREAMING

GUARD: (*Sings.*)

WAKE UP SCREAMING
NO-ONE WILL HEAR
HERE YOUR LIFE WILL BE PAIN AND TENEBRITY
ABANDON HOPE MR WIRELESS CELEBRITY
FROM HERE-ON-IN YOUR HUMILIATION GROWS
SO LET'S START OFF BY REMOVING YOUR CLOTHES

DICK BARTON: (*Sings.*)
> IT'S A NIGHTMARE IT CAN'T BE HAPPENING

GUARD: (*Sings.*)
> FIRST THE TIE, PLEASE

DICK BARTON: (*Sings.*)
> IF I ONLY COULD GET MY HEAD CLEAR

GUARD: (*Sings.*)
> THE JACKET

DICK BARTON: (*Sings.*)
> IT'S A NIGHTMARE, THIS CANNOT BE HAPPENING

GUARD: (*Sings.*)
> THE TROUSERS

DICK BARTON: (*Sings.*)
> I WILL *NOT* TAKE MY TROUSERS OFF HERE!

GUARD: (*Sings.*)
> BARTON, LET'S GET ONE THING CLEAR RIGHT AWAY…

DICK BARTON: (*Sings.*)
> I REFUSE, I REFUSE TO SUBMIT

GUARD: (*Sings.*)
> FROM NOW ON YOU'LL DO AS I SAY

DICK BARTON: (*Sings.*)
> I'M DICK BARTON, THERE MUST BE AN ERROR

GUARD: (*Sings.*)
> IF YOU DON'T

DICK BARTON: (*Sings.*)
> THIS FEELING I FEEL MUST BE TERROR

GUARD: (*Sings.*)
> YOU'LL BE TORN

DICK BARTON: (*Sings.*)
IS THIS REALLY THE END, IS THIS IT?

GUARD: (*Sings.*)
LIMB FROM LIMB

YOU'RE MY PLAYTHING, YOU'LL OBLIGE EVERY WHIM
DON'T LOOK ROUND, THERE IS NO-ONE TO RESCUE YOU

DICK BARTON: (*Sings.*)
A RESCUE WOULD APPEAR OUT OF THE QUESTION
STRANGE FEARS ARISE INSIDE ME

GUARD: (*Sings.*)
NOW ALL THE TABLES ARE TURNED

DICK BARTON: (*Sings.*)
PERHAPS THEY'VE CERTIFIED ME

GUARD: (*Sings.*)
– WHAT FEARS GO THROUGH YOU?

DICK BARTON: (*Sings.*)
DEAR GOD! A FRIEND TO GUIDE ME!

GUARD: (*Sings.*)
AND THIS IS JUST A PREVIEW! YES!

DICK BARTON: (*Sings.*)
THINGS AREN'T GOING WELL

GUARD: (*Sings.*)
ALRIGHT THEN, VERY WELL –

DICK BARTON: (*Sings.*)
AAH.

GUARD: (*Sings.*)
HAVE A TASTE OF HELL!

DICK BARTON: (*Sings.*)
AAH!

The GUARD attempts to strangle DICK BARTON. When the song ends, he awakes from the nightmare. The GUARD is actually trying to wake him.

GUARD: Wakey wakey rise and shine, Mr Barton. Ready to face your first day in Hell?

DICK BARTON: I'm ready for anything you can throw at me.

GUARD: (*Throws a banana at him.*) Weren't ready for that, were you.

BBC ANNOUNCER: And so the torture begins for our hero. Meanwhile, at Barton's office in Wimpole St, the nation's favourite sidekicks, Jock Anderson and Snowy White, begin the process of bagging up the trophies and memories of their heroic past, and prepare the way for their uncertain futures.

Scene 3

DICK BARTON's office.

SNOWY stands by the desk, thinking. MRS HORROCKS is in her bath chair bed contraption. JOCK comes in, his arms loaded with boxes. He looks toward SNOWY, stops, then goes out. JOCK comes in again with another load of boxes. He looks at SNOWY.

JOCK: A lot of memories in this place, eh Snowy?

SNOWY: D'you know, Jock, as I stand here, rooted to the spot, deep in thought, a great drama is being played out before my very eyes, as if it's being projected onto a huge screen in front of me.

JOCK : Really? What is it?

SNOWY: I don't know but it's got some cracking birds in it.

JOCK: Well. Maybe if you were to help me move some of the stuff it might take yer mind off things for a bit.

SNOWY: Nah. It probably wouldn't help. I'm better off standing here.

JOCK: Oh.

JOCK goes off with his boxes. He comes back in.

SNOWY: Poor old Mrs Horrocks.

JOCK: Aye. Look at her. Our long-term homely housekeeper.

SNOWY: Forced into retirement, and she's only eighty-two.

JOCK: Aye. It's good of ye to look after her. Give us a wave, dear.

SNOWY: She's not well at all, y'know.

JOCK: I hardly recognise her.

SNOWY: Me neither.

JOCK: It's like she's a completely different person. Are ye alright dear?

SNOWY: She won't speak to you.

JOCK: No?

SNOWY: Nah. She don't speak to no-one other than the mysterious person with whom she often holds long private phone-calls, and whose name she refuses to divulge.

JOCK : Shame. What do you think they'll replace the programme with when we finally go off the air?

SNOWY: Gawd knows. Some kind of variety show probably. Or a quiz. Or some sort of everyday story of country folk.

JOCK: Aye, probably. Jings! Things are in a right state are they not?

SNOWY: Pound's dropped dramatically.

JOCK : National morale at its lowest since the War.

SNOWY: Cup Final cancelled due to lack of interest.

JOCK: Transport system gone to pot.

SNOWY: That's right. My mate says the other day he went to catch a bus and he waited for ages and then three turned up at regularly spaced intervals. I mean, what's the point of that? What's wrong with a good old fashioned convoy?

JOCK : Don't know what the world's coming to.

SNOWY: Flag's at half-mast at Buckingham Palace 'cause the King's gone to bed and refuses to get up.

JOCK: Och, Snowy, I wish I'd accepted that cushy Police job in the Gorbals when I had the chance. Daphne had always promised to marry me if I took it. I'm at a loss as to what to do. Whoever framed the guvnor must have really known what they were doing. It's tearing us all apart. This must have been a real inside job.

SNOWY: You can bet your bailiff's badgers it was. Whoever done this to the boss must have been pretty desperate to get rid of him.

JOCK: And they must have had inside information. Someone close to the guvnor.

SNOWY: Very close.

They catch each other looking at each other.

They are divided.

BBC ANNOUNCER: Oh dear, folks! Keep an eye out for who's standing at your shoulder, for everybody is a suspect. Who framed Dick Barton? No doubt our hero will begin the task of finding out as he prepares to meet a new colleague and helpmate.

WISBEY / BEDNARCZYK / CRAIG

Scene 4

DICK BARTON's cell.

DICK BARTON sat on his own in his prison uniform. The GUARD looks in.

GUARD: Alright, Barton, stand by yer bed. You've got company. Cell mate coming in. And seeing as how it's yer cellmate's first day and what with you being a celebrity, the guvnor has allowed you tea on the house. (*He hands him a tea pot.*)

DICK BARTON: (*Looks into it.*) How very kind. Thanks. It's got no tea in it.

GUARD: What do you expect? You're in prison now. Only the guvnor gets tea in his tea. You should be grateful it's got milk and water.

DICK BARTON: Of course. Tell the guvnor I thank him from the bottom of my heart.

GUARD: I'd better not. It'll probably make him cry. (*He ushers the new cell mate in.*)

Here you go. Don't have too much fun will you. (*He goes.*) I'm now locking you in.

The door makes a peculiar sound. DICK BARTON looks at his new cell mate.

DICK BARTON: Hallo. You look a bit young for this sort of caper. Juvenile, are you? What's yer name?

CHARLES: Erm. Erm…ah… Charles.

DICK BARTON: Charles.

CHARLES: Yes.

DICK BARTON: That's an odd name for a convict.

CHARLES: Oh. Deadeye Charles.

DICK BARTON: Deadeye Charles.

CHARLES: Yes.

DICK BARTON: Why?

CHARLES: Erm... My eye's dead.

DICK BARTON: Your eye's dead.

CHARLES: Yes.

DICK BARTON: Which one?

CHARLES: Oh. Er. That one. The er, the one on the left.

DICK BARTON: The one of the left.

CHARLES: Yes.

DICK BARTON: The left one then.

CHARLES: Yes.

DICK BARTON: Looks alright to me. In fact it looks quite lively. Must be a ghost. Tell me, what did it die of?

CHARLES: I... I...oh it's all so terribly...!!! (*He feels the pressure and sobs.*)

DICK BARTON: Oh dear oh dear oh dear. There now. Come on, don't cry. Here. Let me dry your eyes. Although I shan't bother with that one because it's quite dead isn't it.

CHARLES laughs at DICK BARTON's little joke. They have a little moment.

Don't worry, Deadeye Charles. I'm going to look after you. We're in this together. We're going to have to stick together like bits of gluey jam on a sticky toffee magnet made of honey from now on. And I don't say that to everybody. (*To himself.*) In fact... I would never say something like that. How odd. (*To CHARLES.*) Understand?

Change
voices —
— clever girl
— Probably
quite scared
but brave.

CHARLES: Yes, sir.

DICK BARTON: You're not really a criminal at all, are you?

CHARLES: No sir.

DICK BARTON: You're just an ordinary down to earth chap like me, eh?

CHARLES: 'Fraid so, sir.

DICK BARTON: What are you in for?

CHARLES: I'd rather not say. I have my father to thank for being in here, sir. Oh, Daddy! I do miss him so!

DICK BARTON: There there. Don't worry. You needn't feel unprotected. I'm your Daddy now. Now listen to me, you young pup. I know you can't say why you're in here, but I've a suspicion you're a victim of circumstance like me. Well. We're in this together. We're going to have to stick together like bits of gluey jam on a sticky toffee magnet made of honey from now on. (*To himself.*) Hang on a minute, I've just said that. I've never repeated myself before. And what's more I'm repeating something linguistically incongruous. Linguistically incongruous? I've never said that before either. (*To CHARLES.*) Would you like to share my pot of tea? Got a cup? You could pour it if you like.

CHARLES pours the tea. It sounds like a champagne bottle being opened and poured.

(*To himself.*) I'm not going mad. I refuse to go mad.

CHARLES: Tell me, sir. What's it like being a hero? Saving the free world and always getting the girl?

DICK BARTON: Ah that's where you've been misinformed, young fellow mi laddy. I know it may be hard to believe, but actually… I never get the girl.

CHARLES: No?

DICK BARTON: No. I always get the girl for someone else. You see, as a national hero I have no time to think of myself. I always have to be there on hand for others. Those are the requirements of the job. Modesty, humility.

CHARLES: A body like a Greek god.

DICK BARTON: That sort of thing.

CHARLES: How thrilling!

DICK BARTON: Not really. All in a day's work. Actually, it's rather lonely. I travel the world insuring a lasting freedom for all. But at the end of it all I drink my cocoa alone, then I go to bed and then I sleep. Alone. You know, it's a rather humbling experience going to sleep knowing that every man, woman and child thinks you're the greatest thing ever to happen to the human race.

CHARLES: Yes, I can see how that would leave one feeling rather insecure.

DICK BARTON: It's an enormous pressure.

CHARLES: Has there never been anyone special in your life?

DICK BARTON: Read this.

CHARLES: What is it?

DICK BARTON: It is a BBC Memo, dated the twenty-seventh of August nineteen forty-seven, outlining the rules by which my adventures are to be written. Basically it tells the writers, producers and all the other monkeys exactly what I can and can't do. It's known as the Special Agent Code. Look at Section Nine. Tells you all you need to know.

CHARLES: *Sex, in the active sense, plays no part in the Barton adventures. This provision does not, rule out the possibility of a decent marriage taking place.*

Well that's alright.

DICK BARTON: Read on.

CHARLES: '*Not personally involving Dick.*' I can see how that would present a problem. So has there never been anyone?

DICK BARTON: There was one. Once.

Dorabella

CHARLES: (Sings.)
WHAT WAS HER NAME?

[handwritten: Amazing Grace]

DICK BARTON: (*Sings.*)
IT'S...DORABELLA.
WE MET AT CAMBRIDGE AT A DANCE
SHE BRUSHED SOME FLUFF FROM MY LAPEL
AND IT WAS LOVE, LOVE AT FIRST GLANCE.

SHE HAD BEAUTY, SHE WAS TRULY SPLENDID
AND HER MIND, HER WIT, ALL OTHER GIRLS TRANSCENDED
WHEN WE – AT LAST – TOOK TO THE FLOOR
I PRAYED TO GOD WE'D DANCE FOR EVERMORE

ONE SINGLE DANCE – AND THEN TO BLIGHT ALL
MY HOPES: 'THERE'S A COLONEL FROM WHITEHALL
HE'S WAITING IN THE COLLEGE HALL –
NO, SIR, PLEASE COME NOW – YOU MUST LEAVE THE BALL'

I SWORE THAT I'D RETURN AND RAN TO SEE THE COLONEL
BUT AS I LEFT I PLEDGED MY LOVE WOULD BE ETERNAL
HOW COULD FATE BRING ME SUCH AS SHE
AND THEN EXTINGUISH ECSTACY?
THAT VERY NIGHT THE KING HAD CALLED ON ME
MY COUNTRY NEEDED ME, AND RIGHT AWAY –

34

SWORN IN AS SPECIAL AGENT BY THE BREAK OF DAY,
FLOWN OVERSEAS BY DAWN'S FIRST LIGHT
WITH NO FAREWELL
THE GIRL WITHOUT WHOM DAY IS NIGHT
MY DORABELL — A

But that's all by the by. I've no time for such matters now.

VOICE: This is the Voice. Would Dick Barton go to the Guvnor's room. Repeat. Dick Barton you will go to the Guvnor's room.

GUARD: (*Enters.*) Well well well, Barton. A chance to thank him in person, eh?

DICK BARTON: Yes. At last! I must have won some sort of appeal! It's my reprieve! I said I wouldn't be in here long. Goodbye, young Charles. You're on yer own now I'm afraid.

CHARLES sobs.

Well, Guard. Lead me to the Governor's office. I'd better get packing.

GUARD: Oh no, Barton. You won't be needing a suitcase where you're going.

DICK BARTON: No?

GUARD: Oh no. You're not going to see Governor Banks.

DICK BARTON: No?

GUARD: No. You're going to see the real guvnor. The man who *really* runs this place. Mister Huge.

CHARLES: I'll come with you. Just in case.

DICK BARTON: Yes. Thanks.

BBC ANNOUNCER: What a nice boy! And so helpful. Meanwhile, homeless and jobless, with the invalid Mrs

35

Horrocks never far from his side, former sidekick Snowy White is not taking things lying down, and he decides to take action in the manner traditional to our plucky friends from London's East End.

Scene 5

A pub.

SNOWY is sat in a pub, nursing the end of a pint. He has MRS HORROCKS with him, in her contraption. There are a few empties in front of him. He's a bit red-faced but not too drunk. JOCK enters, carrying a big rucksack.

JOCK: Snowy.

SNOWY: Oh it's you. Back so soon?

JOCK : I thought I'd find you in here.

SNOWY: Oh did you.

JOCK: Re-acquainting yourself with an old friend, I see.

SNOWY: Well don't worry about me, I'm alright. It's Mrs Horrocks you ought to worry about.

JOCK: How is she?

SNOWY: Not good. She's on her last legs alright and no mistake. To be honest I'll be surprised if she makes it through to the end of the episode. Not that you care.

JOCK: Och there's no need for that. I've been busy. So I've come to say goodbye before I leave.

SNOWY: Oh, leaving are you? You've only just got back.

JOCK: I know, but I've had some exciting news. By a strange, but nonetheless quite handy coincidence, the cushy police job in the Gorbles I've been after has become open again. It's a very tragic tale. It seems that while I was visiting the area to check on Granny McNair and to have an interview for the job as assistant Chief, the Chief himself had died in a tragic accident.

SNOWY: Eh?

JOCK: Aye. It's a mystery alright. It seems he was out picking loganberries on his own in the middle of the night, when he suddenly died of a mysterious gunshot wound to the back of the head. But the good news is I have been offered the unfortunate man's job. So that's why I've come back to London, to put my affairs in order before I move up there for good.

SNOWY: Oh. Well I'm very pleased for you. I suppose you'll be able to marry Daphne now.

JOCK: Aye. I feel very sorry for the dead man's family, but it is rather a useful coincidence as far as my life's concerned.

SNOWY: So. This 'accident'. I hate to throw poison on yer porridge, but in my experience a gunshot wound to the head is usually the result of some sort of shooting incident.

JOCK: Och no. Things like that never happen in the Gorbals. Anyway, I've looked into the matter personally and it was definitely an accident. The Chief had taken his shotgun with him to keep the moths away, probably carrying it on his back, and the trigger had got caught on a bramble and blown the back of his head off. A simple, all-too-common, rural accident.

MARY the barmaid enters. Her actions do not connect with the sound. She leaves.

JOCK: What happened there?

They look at each other. Then try to shake it off.

BBC ANNOUNCER: How curious. Meanwhile, back in Dartmoor, our hero Dick Barton prepares to meet a new foe, or will he turn out to be a new friend?

He arrives at the cell of the

Scene 6

infamous Mr Huge

Mr HUGE's cell.

DICK BARTON is ushered into the cell. He meets PETER, the Professor.

PETER: Ah Mr Barton. Welcome. Make yourself at home. After all, you're going to be here an awfully long time.

DICK BARTON: You! So it's you who's behind all this. I might have known. I thought I detected the foul stench of… I don't know you, do I?

PETER: I don't believe so. I am Peter, but I am known as the Professor.

DICK BARTON: Peter the Professor, eh? So you're in charge here. Well let me just set down a few rules for you, my friend. Let me make this clear…

PETER: You can save your breath, Mr Barton. I'm not the guvnor. Mr Huge is the biggest criminal mind in this prison and he will be back shortly.

DICK BARTON: Where's he gone?

PETER: Classified information, Mr Barton. I'm sure you understand.

DICK BARTON: So who are you then?

PETER: I'm the clever one who can get you anything, anything you want from the outside world. Just name it and I can get it. That sort of thing.

DICK BARTON: Really?

PETER: Oh yes. Any requests?

DICK BARTON: Yes I have actually. I'd like you to get me a rock hammer.

PETER: A rock hammer, eh?

DICK BARTON: Yes please. And a Sten gun with five hundred rounds, a box of grenades, a pickaxe, some mountaineering equipment, a Spitfire and an army of sharks.

PETER: Oh yes? Planning an escape, eh?

DICK BARTON: (*Very deadpan.*) Dash it, who told you.

PETER: I have friends in high places.

DICK BARTON: Let me guess. You're a tennis umpire.

PETER: Very witty, Mr Barton. I do like a good joke.

DICK BARTON: I'm not in here for your amusement.

HUGE: (*At the door.*) No, Mr Barton. Quite right. Not his. Mine.

PETER: Dick Barton, may I introduce my boss, the big man himself, Mr Huge.

DICK BARTON: So! At long last. Didn't take you long to crawl out of your cage, did it? Well if you think I'm going to… I don't know you either do I?

HUGE: Not directly, no. Alright, Professor Peter, you can relax. Now that Mr Barton's here, I think it's time to meet my trusty sidekicks. Come in, boys.

Enter LAUGHING JAKE.

HUGE: This is Laughing Jake. I'll explain why in a minute. Say hello, Laughing Jake.

JAKE: Hello, Laughing Jake.

He laughs for far too long at this pathetic joke.

39

DICK BARTON: I see. I think we can dispense with the explanation.

HUGE: He may not look much to you, but trust me. He is feared and renowned throughout the criminal world for his savage cruelty and massive over-reactions to poor quality music hall routines.

BOB: (*Voice off.*) Sorry I'm late!

HUGE: Ah, here comes my other sidekick, Late Bob.

Enter LATE BOB.

BOB: I got held up, there was a problem on the Northern Line, me dog ate me homework and I had to take me gran to hospital.

HUGE: Not to worry, Bob. You're here now. Good old Bob. Always late. So. What do you think of my trusty sidekicks, eh? Bet you wish you had a sidekick. It'll be a long time until you find one in here I'm afraid. Oh yes. Eh, lads?

DICK BARTON: On the contrary. I already have.

All are agasp.

HUGE: What?

PETER: Already?

DICK BARTON: Yes. Come in, Charles.

Enter CHARLES. They all stare at him.

HUGE: I say. Who's this?

DICK BARTON: This is Charles.

CHARLES: Deadeye Charles.

DICK BARTON: Deadeye Charles.

JAKE: Deadeye Charles?

CHARLES: Deadeye Charles.

BOB: What sort of a name's that?

CHARLES: It's a nickname.

PETER: Yes but why Deadeye?

CHARLES: My eye's dead.

PETER: Looks alright to me.

DICK BARTON: So. Mr Big.

HUGE: I think you'll find it's Huge, Mr Barton. I can't tell you how much it pleases me.

DICK BARTON: What?

HUGE: To see you in here.

DICK BARTON: Oh that. Of course you know I'm innocent. I was framed.

BOB: It doesn't look that dead to me.

HUGE: Keep up, Bob. Of course. How very dull. Society is full of innocent people. There is only one thing more vulgar than innocence…

DICK BARTON: Oh dear. A master criminal with an Oscar Wilde complex.

HUGE: It suits me very much that you're in here, Barton. For two reasons.

DICK BARTON: There are always two reasons with you greedy criminal types. You're never happy with yer fair share. Alright. Let's have the first.

HUGE: With you out of the way it'll be much easier for me to run things in the outside world.

41

DICK BARTON: Aha! But surely if I'm out of the way, so are you. How can you possibly run the outside world when you're in here? Hadn't thought of that, had you? Not feeling so clever now, eh?

HUGE: Oh how very naive. To be naive is to be ignorant and to be ignorant is to be dull. Society is full of naive people. There is only one thing more vulgar than naivety…

DICK BARTON: I do hope there's a point to all this.

HUGE: Who do you think was really behind the case of the Maharaja and the angry duck?

DICK BARTON: Let me guess. You?

HUGE: The very same. And where do you think the idea to kidnap the Duchess of Mulberry came from?

DICK BARTON: I see. Very clever.

HUGE: And who do you think stole your housekeeper's bike?

DICK BARTON: You cad! Alright. I think I'm getting the picture. What's the other reason for wanting me in here?

HUGE: With you by my side, with your knowledge, your experience, your ability to get out of tricky situations and confound your enemies, I will, I mean we, will be the most potent criminal force on Earth. Think about it.

DICK BARTON: I'll never join with you and your evil clan, Mr Stout.

HUGE: Huge! Huge! It's Huge, I tell you!

DICK BARTON: Don't flatter yourself. You might be huge to your minions, but you're a minnow in the grand scheme.

HUGE: Oh, you know about it already?

DICK BARTON: What?

HUGE: The Grand Scheme. My plan.

DICK BARTON: Why of course I know about it. But, just remind me of the details.

HUGE: Impossible. Even I don't know the details. This scheme is so brilliant and so top secret that I am even withholding information from myself. I have always been of the opinion that one thing is certain. It will bring this pathetic little country to its knees.

DICK BARTON: Oh yes? And what do you call this great plot of yours? There's usually some idiotic title.

HUGE: An idiotic title is better than no title at all. But not this time. This time it's brilliant. This time I'm calling it 'The Great Plot.'

Hurrahs and general approval from the minions.

DICK BARTON: Not particularly inventive.

HUGE: Oh yes? Think you can do better, eh? How very vulgar. Come on then. Let's hear it.

DICK BARTON: Alright. 'The Flight Of The Phoenix.'

BOB: That's quite good actually.

JAKE: It's catchy.

HUGE: Yes, but it's wrong. The plan doesn't have anything to do with flight, and there are no phoenixes in it.

JAKE: Doesn't matter. If it's catchy it'll sell.

HUGE: I don't want it to be catchy and I'm not trying to sell it. I want it to be a well kept secret and expertly executed.

JAKE: George Formby's 'When I'm Cleaning Windows' was catchy. That sold loads.

HUGE: Yes, but it wasn't a well kept secret though, was it.

PETER: Sadly.

DICK BARTON: It wasn't particularly well executed either if I remember rightly.

PETER: Neither was Formby, more's the pity.

HUGE: Enough! I want you to join me, Barton.

DICK BARTON: Never.

Pause.

BOB: Oh, go on.

DICK BARTON: No.

BOB: I'll be yer best friend.

HUGE: You will join me, Barton. It's only a matter of time. I have always been of the opinion that time is a fascist concept. Come on. Live a little. It's dangerous, exciting, exhilarating. Be bad. Be really wicked.

The Wicked Life

HUGE: (*Sings.*)
YOU'LL FIND THE WICKED LIFE IS WONDERFUL,
YOU'LL FIND THE WICKED PATH DIVINE.
YOU GET YOUR SACKS MARKED 'SWAG' WITH PLUNDER FULL
YOU GET TO HARBOUR THOUGHTS MALIGN
THREE LITTLE WORDS SUFFICE AS EPIGRAPH
WELL, LOOK AT JAKE – WE HAVE A LAUGH!

HUGE/JAKE/BOB (*Sing.*)
WE HAVE A LAUGH (WE HAVE A LAUGH.)
WE HAVE A LAUGH (WE HAVE A LAUGH.)
OH, MR BARTON, HAVE A LAUGH!

Repeat.

HUGE: (*Sings.*)
THE CAMARAD'RIE SETS YOU REELING
WE ALL BELONG BEHIND THESE BARS.
THE GUTTER'S REALLY SO APPEALING
FOR WE ARE LOOKING AT THE STARS!
EMBRACE THE WAYS OF MEPHISTOPHELES
YOU KNOW YOU COULD — OH, JOIN US PLEASE!

HUGE/JAKE/BOB (*Sing.*)
OH JOIN US PLEASE (OH JOIN US PLEASE.)
OH JOIN US PLEASE (OH JOIN US PLEASE.)
OH MR BARTON, JOIN US PLEASE

Wild x 2nd
So obvious

Repeat.

Instrumental and dance chorus, during which…

DICK BARTON: (*Grabbing CHARLES who has been joining in.*) Dash it, Charles, I thought you were batting for my team.

CHARLES: What?? Oh, I see! No, I am on your side, but you can't beat them by force. You have to infiltrate their ranks, you know, form our own fifth column. Break them down from within.

DICK BARTON: I don't think I could cut the mustard. I could never get the hang of this evil criminal malarkey. I'm not…

CHARLES: You have to. You have to convince them!

CHARLES is whisked back into the dance. DICK BARTON makes an attempt. Towards the end of the dance HUGE approaches him.

— *Oh join us repeat*

HUGE: Oh, Mr Barton, if you would only join us. Imagine our combined strength. Think what we could achieve together! (*Sings.*)

TOGETHER, THEY COULD NOT POLICE US
TOGETHER WE COULD RULE THE EARTH
TOGETHER WE'D BE RICH AS CROESUS
TOGETHER – THINK WHAT WE'D BE WORTH!
MY PLAN, MY PLAN WILL MAKE US EMPERORS
IN TERMS OF STREETS – RIGHT UP YOURS!

HUGE/JAKE/BOB (*Sing.*)
IT'S RIGHT UP YOURS (IT'S RIGHT UP YOURS.)
IT'S RIGHT UP YOURS (IT'S RIGHT UP YOURS.)
OH MR BARTON, RIGHT UP YOURS!

Repeat.

HUGE: Well, boys. I think it's time to bring out the 'Prison Tea'! That should turn him!

ALL: Yes, hooray etc… Prison tea! Prison Tea!

DICK BARTON: Wait a minute. What's in this 'Prison Tea'? Alcohol? Some kind of mind-altering narcotic?

BOB: No. It's just tea. But we call it Prison Tea to make it sound more exciting.

HUGE: Don't listen to him. It's actually a highly dangerous cocktail…

BOB: Of blended teas from around the world.

HUGE: Shut up!… It's lethal. Well, not actually lethal obviously, but it's pretty deadly. Well no it's not deadly either or we'd all be dead but it's mean stuff, I can tell you, and only the most hardened criminal would drink it.

DICK BARTON: A real connoisseur, eh?

HUGE: On the contrary. A connoisseur finds the quality in a wine. I, on the other hand, prefer to sit back and let the wine find the quality in me.

DICK BARTON: But this is tea.

HUGE: And what a tea it is.

DICK BARTON: Then bring it on. I've got a raging thirst.

CHARLES: Careful, sir. It might actually turn you evil.

DICK BARTON: I've no choice. I have to risk it, Charles. For the sake of the free world.

HUGE: Pour him a cup, lads! Let's see what kind of guts he's got.

Somebody pours some tea. It sounds completely different.

DICK BARTON: Pssst! Charles!

CHARLES: What, sir?

DICK BARTON: Did you notice that?

CHARLES: Yes sir.

DICK BARTON: Thank god you heard it too. I'm not going mad. I think I may have an idea. Right. Let's see what this stuff's all about.

He drinks some of the tea. He turns around to see that the criminals all have noses and glasses on or something and they're all trying to make him feel woozy.

HUGE: Wooooh wooooooh! Feeling queezy, Mr Barton? Notice anything strange lippa lippa bang quoodle dwap?

DICK BARTON: No, I'm fine.

They continue trying to freak him out. 'The pips.' Everybody suddenly freezes

VOICE: This is the Voice. Telephone call for Mr Huge. Repeat, telephone call for Mr Huge.

HUGE: Oh dash it, I'm late! There is only one thing more vulgar than being late… (*Goes to exit, he stops by the door.*)

Goodbye Charles. Charmed to meet you. Absolutely… absolutely charmed.

47

CHARLES: Wish I could say the same. — *Sickly sweet.*

HUGE storms off, muttering Wildean things.

DICK BARTON: What's so important about this phone call that he has to leave like that?

BOB: It's probably the VIP.

DICK BARTON: The VIP?

PETER: Careful, Bob.

BOB: Oh, sorry.

DICK BARTON: Who's the VIP?

PETER: We don't know. We only know that he or she is something to do with the Great Plot. Mr H always becomes quite disturbed when he hears the voice of the VIP.

BOB: Like me when I hear Brian speaking.

DICK BARTON: Who's Brian?

BOB: My fluffy little gerbil.

DICK BARTON: Yes I can see how that could be disturbing.

BOB: It certainly is. He's been dead for two years…

DICK BARTON: Good. He deserved it.

They all wince through their teeth.

BOB: Aw!

PETER: Nasty.

JAKE: No need for that.

DICK BARTON: Is somebody going to pour me some more of this tea or am I going to have to come over there and take action?

Tea is poured very quickly.

Bob — I'll do it . . .

BBC ANNOUNCER: Oh my word! Careful, Dick! Is the evil tea having an effect already? Can it really turn a good man bad? Can there really be a tea more dangerous than the liquid litter they serve here in the BBC Canteen?

Phone rings.

Meanwhile over in Whitehall, our hero's ex-boss, Colonel Gardener, receives what can only be described as a mysterious telephone call.

Scene 7

COLONEL GARDENER's office.

COLONEL GARDENER: Hello? I beg your pardon? You'd like to do what to me?... Who is this? Stop panting like that, I can't make out what you're... Oh it's you, Mother... What do you want? You've eaten my what? Oh no! Not my best ones? The ones I keep for special occasions? But I've only just had them taken in at the waist. Well you'll just have to go to the tailor's and get me a new pair, won't you. (*Puts the phone down.*)

*De*crease the dose, I said.

The phone rings again.

Hello? Ah Jean, very good. Thank you, Jean. Send him straight in.

Enter SNOWY with MRS HORROCKS.

Ah, Mr White.

SNOWY: Cor blimey. *Mister* White. *Mister* White, eh? I wish my old ma could hear you say that.

COLONEL GARDENER: I'm sure you do. Now. Please. Take a seat.

SNOWY: Thank you.

COLONEL GARDENER: How is Mrs Horrocks?

SNOWY: She don't talk to me much nowadays. She can talk though. In fact, I was telling Jock only the other day as how she often has to take rather long private phone calls from a mysterious person whose name she refuses to divulge.

Pause.

COLONEL GARDENER: Really. Well at least we can trust her not to pass on any state secrets that may be discussed during this high priority confidential meeting. Mister White, I have called you here on a very serious matter indeed.

SNOWY: I know.

COLONEL GARDENER: Have you any idea why I've called you in here today?

SNOWY: Yes.

COLONEL GARDENER: I thought not. As a top secret matter only those with access to…beg pardon?

SNOWY: Did I say yes? I meant no.

COLONEL GARDENER: Ah. You will probably not be aware that it has been decided by the powers that be that a temporary replacement for Mr Barton should be put in place as soon as possible in order to minimise the risk of foreign devilment.

SNOWY: I know.

COLONEL GARDENER: Neither will you be aware, that it…how?

SNOWY: I read it in the Times personal column.

COLONEL GARDENER: Good God. That paper really doesn't have the elitist readership it used to have, does it. I can see we're going to have to find some other way of circulating secret data from now on. (*Picks up phone.*) Jean, we need a chat. (*Puts it down.*)

SNOWY: I also have access to most of the top secret files. Have had for years. It's amazing what a secretary will do for half a pound of elderberry fudge.

COLONEL GARDENER: (*Picks up phone.*) Jean, we really need a chat. (*Puts it down.*) I shan't beat about the bush, Mr White. For this job we need somebody who knows the duties of a special agent inside out, who has stability, solidity, credibility, insight, good in a fight, experience and a Macintosh. So. Tell me. Before we move on, what qualities do you think you have that make you an ideal candidate for the job?

SNOWY: (*After some thought.*) I know how to work the phone.

COLONEL GARDENER: That's good enough for me. The job's yours. Got a Macintosh?

SNOWY: No.

COLONEL GARDENER: Not to worry. Those are Barton's old hat and coat on the stand there. I was going to burn them, but if they fit, you might as well have them. I hope you understand you will only be filling this post as a stop-gap until they appoint a real successor. It's a great responsibility but one I'm sure you can handle. Do you mind letting yourself out?

SNOWY: Why? Where are you going?

Pause.

COLONEL GARDENER: You don't need to know.

SNOWY: Oh. Well have a nice time. It'll be quite fun having you as my immediate superior.

COLONEL GARDENER: Oh no. You'll have your own. New chap. It was always the case that as long as Britain needed Barton, Barton would need me. Now that he's gone there's no reason for me to hang around. So I'm going to…so I'm going. Enjoy your new job. And remember, if ever you need me, don't bother to call, because I shan't be here. (*He exits.*)

SNOWY: (*Tries on the hat and mac. They don't fit at all.*) It fits like a glove. Blimey. Well done, Snowy me old son. (*In a Bartonesque voice.*) Yes. Well done, Snowy. I knew I could rely on you. (*As himself.*) Blimey!

BBC ANNOUNCER: Blimey indeed! Our hero has only been away for a short while, and already they're jumping in his grave like children at a swimming pool! Concurrently, there is a new horrible twist to our gripping tale. Listeners of a nervous disposition should cork up their ears as it seems our hero is about to learn the real meaning of the word 'torture'. Back in prison, in the boiler room, Mr Huge's plot to turn Barton bad has taken a turn for the worse…

Scene 8

The boiler room in the prison.

The place is steamy, smoky, with odd sparks, hisses and bizarre noises. There are signs everywhere telling of dangers of various kinds. DICK BARTON is tied, stripped to the waist, in a chair. The gang are around him. It is a very menacing scene. PETER is holding a drill to DICK BARTON's head.

HUGE: Mr Barton. My patience is at an end. I'll ask you once more. Will you, Dick Barton, join me, Jefferypold Huge in criminal despicability? Will you help me,

52

advise me, give me all of Britain's top defensive secrets and be my partner in crime as long as we both shall thrive?

DICK BARTON: (*Thinks about it for a bit.*) No.

HUGE: Ooh it's a good guess but I'm afraid it's not the answer we were looking for. (*He clicks his fingers.*)

The lads tighten the screws, as it were.

DICK BARTON: Stop! What's the point of all this? Do you expect me to talk?

HUGE: No, Mr Barton, I expect you to dance! Music!

JAKE switches on a wireless. It is playing 'When I'm Cleanin' Windows'. They all start to dance.

DICK BARTON: Stop! Please stop! Alright alright! Just please stop!

They stop.

Give me more time. Please. I need more time.

HUGE: Very well, Mr Barton. I think you know the score by now. You have one hour to perform a despicable act of inhumanity of my choice, thus showing your willingness to join me. This is your mission. By the end of that hour I want to see, personally hand-delivered by you, the prison cat, Mister Snuffles, killed…

The lads gasp.

…stuffed…

The lads gasp again.

…and mounted in this position. (*He poses.*)

Big reaction to this ghastly display.

And I want its tail to wag! The tails never wag! I hate it! I must have a wagging tail!

DICK BARTON: But how am I supposed to do that?

HUGE: That, Mr Barton, is up to you. One hour. Open the box of death!

The lads open a fuse box. It sparkles and spits and looks very dangerous indeed.

Nasty, isn't it? Forty thousand volts. Well if you don't comply, in there is where we're going to force you to put your hand, or anything else that takes my fancy. It'll look just like a naughty little suicide. Still, I have always been of the opinion that a naughty suicide is better than no suicide at all. There is only one thing more vulgar than a naughty little suicide. Do you understand me? One hour. Or you will suffer the most excruciatingly slow death you have ever suffered. Well. You know what I mean. Come on, boys. I think we've done enough.

They leave.

PETER: Psst. My friend. Take this. You'll be needing it. (*He hands him a small oddly-shaped mechanism.*)

DICK BARTON: Thanks, Peter. What is it?

PETER: It's a mechanism to make the tail wag. You see, you implant this end of it into the part of the cat from which it delivers its little curly carpet parcels, switch it on, and hey presto, the tail will wag like the poor moggy was still alive.

DICK BARTON: (*Trying not to swear.*) By the five fiendish fat-headed farmers of Fife! That's disgusting. But it might come in handy. Thanks, Peter. One thing. How can you guarantee it works?

PETER: Oh it'll work alright.

DICK BARTON: Good.

PETER: It always has before. (*He exits.*)

DICK BARTON: Good… Ooh! (*He drops it on the floor in disgust and then slumps into a depression. He begins to pray.*)

Barton's Prayer

DICK BARTON: (*Sings.*)

OUR FATHER, WHO ART IN HEAVEN,
HALLO… BARTON HERE.
I KNOW YOU KNOW, IT'S JUST I COULD FORSEE
YOU MIGHT BE SOMEWHAT BUSY WITHOUT ME
I DON'T WANT TO JUMP THE QUEUE
BUT THINGS ARE GETTING SLIGHTLY DESPERATE
AND I'M IN A BIT OF A STEW

I'VE ALWAYS BEEN A ONE – AS WELL YOU KNOW –
TO CUT THE MUSTARD, MUCK IN, SHARP AS GINGER,
AND WHEN ALL'S SAID AND DONE…
SELF PITY ISN'T ME, I AM NO WHINGER, *BUT*
I HAVE TO SAY, I WOULDN'T MIND IF YOU COULD
HELP A LITTLE
NOT MY WILL, BUT THINE LORD. BUT GIVE ME A
SIGN, LORD.

ONE SIMPLE SIGN!
AND AS I SAY, WITHOUT ME 'ON THE BEAT'
I DARESAY YOU'RE FLAT OUT, RUSHED OFF YOUR FEET.
I DON'T WANT TO BLEAT OR WHINE
BUT IT WOULD BE DIVINE
IF YOU'D REPLY TO THIS PRAYER OF MINE –
JUST A SIGN!

Tumbling out of a pipe comes a package.

That was quick. Benefits of having a direct line I suppose. Thanks very much. Let's see what we've got here. There's a note. 'Dear Mr Barton. This deadly contraption will aid your escape. Best of luck. From a Well Wisher.' Let's have a look then.

(*He pulls out a rubber duck.*) A rubber duck? This can't be it. Wait, there's more. 'Congratulations. You are now the owner of your very own Dudley the Deadly Duck. Squeeze his belly in the face of your enemies and he will emit a chemical cloud which will temporarily blind them within BBC guidelines, leaving no lasting ill effects, thus giving you time to escape. Only one tiny squirt needed, so one duckfull will be enough for a hundred squirts.' Ingenious! Thank you, whoever you are. Come on, Barton. Time for this little Phoenix to fly. Well. Here goes. Guard! Guard!

GUARD: (*Enters.*) Lucky for you I was lurking within earshot. What can I do for you?

DICK BARTON: Well for starters you can take that! (*Squirts it in his face. Nowt comes out.*)

GUARD: Take what? (*He exits.*)

DICK BARTON: Oh. Nothing. Hang on a minute. I might have known. 'Chemical cloud not included.'

DICK BARTON ECHO: (*Voice over.*) *Am I to leap to safety, clear my name and win the day or…no…surely you're not going to…? What's to happen to me?*

LORD REITH ECHO: (*Voice over.*) *That, Barton, is up to God, the Scriptwriters…and you.*

DICK BARTON: God, the scriptwriters and you. One down, two to go, eh, your Almightiness? Wait! What's that up there? It looks like some sort of grate. And if I'm not mistaken it leads to the laundry room. If I could just get up there I could…no, don't be ridiculous. It's too dangerous… All the more reason to try. Here goes!

He tries to climb a pipe but is thrown off by electricity. He falls unconscious. Lights out. Music.

The lights come back up. Lots of smoke. The ANGEL is helping him to come round.

ANGEL: There there now. Whoops a daisy. Looks like somebody's had a nasty fall. Can I help you up?

DICK BARTON: Ah. Yes. Thanks. Don't know what happened there. I must have…who are you?

ANGEL: Oh, nobody really. Just a friend. My name's Terrence.

DICK BARTON: I see. Don't tell me. You're a trainee angel and you want me to help you get your wings.

ANGEL: Oh no no no no no no. Oh no. I've already got my wings. I just don't like to wear them out. I haven't finished paying for them yet, you see. Oh no. It's not my wings. They're fine. It's this little fella. — my lyre, all the angels have one.

(*Pulls a lyre out of its bag.*) I just can't get the hang of this thing at all. No sir. Very tricky. Do you know anything about music?

DICK BARTON: Enough to get by.

ANGEL: Good. Then maybe you can help me. You see I just can't find F sharp anywhere. Could you tell me where I can find F sharp?

DICK BARTON: It's between F and G.

ANGEL: Oh I see. Right here? (*Plays.*)

DICK BARTON: That's the fella.

ANGEL: Well thank you. Now that you've helped me, I can help you. Would you like me to show you what the world would be like if you hadn't been born?

DICK BARTON: Not really.

ANGEL: Oh. Well then I guess I must have the wrong place. I'll make my own way out. Been nice talking to ya.

DICK BARTON: Wait!

ANGEL: Oh? OK. I'll wait. What is it, sonny?

DICK BARTON: You could do me one favour. I know you can't help me to escape or anything, but there is one thing you could do.

ANGEL: Now, now just you name it, Sonny Jim, and I'll see what I can do.

DICK BARTON: You could show me what things are like now, without me. What my friends are up to. That sort of thing.

ANGEL: Oh OK. Yes, I guess I could do that for you.

DICK BARTON: Poor things; I should imagine they must be frightfully unhappy and somewhat aimless without me there.

ANGEL: Oh, I should imagine they are. Shall we take a look?…

Angel Vision Sequence

JOCK: (*Sings.*)

OCH, MA LIFE HAS NEVER BEEN SAE GRAND,

I'M HAPPY IN MA WORK

MA WEE LASS AND I WILL SOON RUN HAND

IN HAND DOWN TO THE KIRK

SINCE DAPHNE'S FATHER HAS ALLOWED

I'VE BOUGHT HER RINGS AND BAUBLES

I'VE A WELL-PAID JOB, I FEEL SAE PROUD —

POLICE CHIEF OF THE GORBALS!

DICK BARTON: I never knew he had it in him.

ANGEL: Are you impressed?

DICK BARTON: I'm something ending with 'pressed'. Move on. Let's see what Snowy's up to. Crying his little cockney heart out, I expect.

ANGEL: Something like that...

SNOWY: (*Sings.*)

I'M IN A RIGHT TWO-AND-EIGHT, BUT IT'S GREAT
I AM NOW A SPECIAL AGENT
AND I HAVEN'T HAD SUCH BLOODY FUN
FOR A LONG, LONG WHILE
(WHO WOULD HAVE THOUGHT? GOR BLIMEY!)

GO FOR A WALK DOWN THE STREET AND I MEET
ALL THE FANS – I'M ALL THE RAGE
TRY TO SATISFY ALL THEIR DEMANDS FOR AN
AUTOGRAPH – WITH A CHEERY SMILE

YOU COULD NOT BELIEVE THE WAY I FEEL
(HAVIN' A BALL!)
HAVE TO PINCH MYSELF TO PROVE IT'S REAL
(THEN COMES A CALL –)
CALLED UPON TO SOLVE THE LATEST CRIMES
(BESTEST OF ALL –)
GET ME PICTURE IN THE RADIO TIMES – OI!

END OF THE DAY – WHEN IT COMES – OFF TO MUM'S
AND SHE COOKS ME UP A DINNER
SAYS SHE'S EVER SO PROUD AND SLIPS INTO
HER NEW MINK
(AND THEN IT'S DOWN THE BOOZER.)

THERE IN THE SNUG IT IS JUG AFTER JUG –
BLOODY HELL, THIS JOB'S A WINNER –
I GET BLADDERED EACH NIGHT
AND BECAUSE I'M FAMOUS I...NEVER BUY A DRINK.
OI!

DICK BARTON: One soon finds out who one's friends are, doesn't one. Surely the Colonel's on my side?

ANGEL: Only one way to find out…

COLONEL GARDENER: (*Sings.*)

IN WORLD WAR TWO I STARTED WELL –
COMMANDER OF A REGIMENT, BUT THEN, OH HELL
FROM ONE MISTAKE MY TROUBLE STEMS:
I MARCHED THE BLOODY REGIMENT INTO THE THAMES
(HE MARCHED ETC…)

A MOMENTARY LAPSE, IT WAS NOT MY FAULT
I WAS 'CHATTING' TO A PRIVATE AND DID NOT SAY 'HALT'
(A MOMENTARY LAPSE ETC…)

MY LIFE THEN GREW YET MORE GROTESQUE
BARRED FROM ACTIVE SERVICE, STUCK BEHIND A DESK
AS A MILITARY MAN I GREW SO GLUM
TO A 'MINOR INDISCRETION' I DID SUCCUMB
(TO A MINOR ETC…)

ONE MINOR INDISCRETION, OR THEREABOUTS
WITH A GRENADIER, A WHIPPET AND A POUND OF SPROUTS
(ONE MINOR ETC…)

THE POWERS THAT BE MADE SUCH A FUSS
THE THINGS THEY SAID WERE REALLY RATHER VENOMOUS
THE MINISTER MADE AN AWFUL STINK
THEN SUDDENLY WENT QUIET, SAYING 'LET ME THINK…
(THEN SUDDENLY ETC…)

…YOU CAN KEEP YOUR DESK AND RANK' SAID HE
'BUT FROM NOW ON YOUR SECONDED TO THE BBC'.
(YOU CAN KEEP YOUR ETC…)

SO THINGS JUST WENT FROM BAD TO WORSE
WHAT APPEARED AS A BLESSING WAS, IN FACT, A CURSE
THE MINISTER'S WORDS WERE SUBTERFUGE:
IN FACT, HE WAS DEMOTING ME TO BARTON'S STOOGE
(IN FACT ETC….)

BARTON GETS HIS MAN, SOLVES CRIMES, HAS CLASS
AND IT'S ME WHO STANDS BESIDE HIM LOOKING LIKE AN ARSE
(BARTON GETS ETC...)

BUT HE'S IN DISGRACE AND...NOW THIS IS INDISCREET,
MY REHABILITATION WOULD APPEAR COMPLETE
HE'S IN PRISON, AND I'M GOING SOMEWHERE PLUSH
DOING SOMETHING – I WOULD TELL YOU, BUT IT'S SO HUSH-HUSH!
(DOING SOMETHING ETC...)

ALL'S FORGIVEN AND FORGOTTEN, SO IT WOULD SEEM –
EVEN THAT 'MISUNDERSTANDING' IN THE GENTS IN CHEAM!
(ALL'S FORGIVEN ETC...)

JOCK/SNOWY/COLONEL GARDENER: (*Sing.*)
OUR LIVES HAVE NEVER BEEN SO GREAT
EVERY DAY GIVES US ANOTHER CAUSE TO CELEBRATE!

DICK BARTON: Well thanks for that. You've really cheered me up.

ANGEL: Not at all. I'll let myself out. Wish I'd brought my wings now. Be an awful lot easier to fly home. Oh well. Goodbye.

DICK BARTON: Goodbye.

ANGEL: Oh. There is one last thing.

DICK BARTON: Yes?

ANGEL: I'm granting you three wishes. Anything you like. You can make them whenever you please.

DICK BARTON: Well I might as well make them now. Anything I like, you say?

ANGEL: Yep.

DICK BARTON: Anything in the world, all I have to do is wish for it?

ANGEL: Absolutely.

DICK BARTON: Alright. Well let's start with world peace, an end to poverty and freedom for all mankind. When can I expect to receive those?

ANGEL: Now you're being silly.

DICK BARTON: *I'm* being silly?! Now just you listen to me. I don't know who you really are, but I've put up with a lot since I came in here and I haven't complained once and I have to warn you my patience is just beginning, *just beginning* to lapse. Now unless you have something useful to offer me like a way out of here, which, if you really had that kind of power, you would have done in the first place, I suggest you leave. Actually, come to think of it, I do have one wish that only you could make come true…

ANGEL: No need, I'm well ahead of you. I'll see myself out. (*Exits.*)

DICK BARTON: Well, Barton old chap. Looks like this really is it. I'll never understand why everybody has forsaken me. Including you. (*God.*) But if my death means that one person lives a better life, then so be it. I must make that sacrifice. I just wish I could find some inspiration from somewhere.

Ting! – on the harp. Enter PETER, agitated.

PETER: Mr Barton, Mr Barton! I have something for you, to aid your escape. I've brought this to you at great personal risk to myself. A brilliant new invention of mine. Take this with you and you'll be able to contact anybody you want from wherever you are. (*He brings in a large object covered with a sheet.*)

May I present the latest thing in communications. I admit it needs a little work, but I think you'll find it most useful. I call it…the mobile telephone! (*He unveils a massive phone with straps on it.*)

You see? All you do is strap it to your back and you can carry it with you anywhere. Try it.

He puts it on.

You see? Now you can call people from wherever you are. In a field, on a train. All you have to do is…oh wait. There's the battery. (*He brings in a giant battery.*) It quite handy it being on wheels! (*smug*)

I'll just plug that in. There we go. Then all you need to do is hold up the aerial like so, and make your call. Simple. Try it.

DICK BARTON: (*Into phone.*) Hello? Hello?… Hello? (*Gives the receiver to PETER.*) 'Network busy, please try later.' Oh well. Thanks for trying. Oh, and this is for you. Read it when you get a private moment. It may be of some help. Goodbye Peter

PETER takes the note and exits as CHARLES enters.

An Charles! Thank heavens you're here! They'll be coming for me in a minute. We've got to get out of this place if it's the last thing we ever do.

CHARLES: Wait! I've been doing some research. Benny the Bosher, who works in the post room, has been keeping an eye out for me and he's discovered something quite interesting. Ever since you arrived he's noticed that there have been letters regularly leaving here for three destinations. Wimpole St.

DICK BARTON: But that's my old address.

CHARLES: Exactly. The Gorbals.

DICK BARTON: The Gorbals. Let's think now. The Gorbals the Gorbals the Gorbals. Jock! I knew it Yes. And the next?

CHARLES: Brace yourself. There have been letters sent from here...to the script editing department of the BBC!

Music sting. Da da dah!

DICK BARTON: I thought as much. That explains the bizarre sound effects.

CHARLES: What about the bad editing?

DICK BARTON: Yes! Not to mention the repetition, spelling mistakes and poor quality jokes and repetition. Looks like the Great Plot may already be underway. We haven't a moment to lose. Quick!

Pause.

CHARLES: What?

DICK BARTON: Don't know. For the love of Pete, Charles. My hour is almost up and I've no means of escape. If I don't think of something soon they're going to come back and stick my dainty digits into that dirty box of tricks that's crackling and spitting away over there. And what's more, I'm so thirsty I could drink a pint of camel spit.

CHARLES: Wait, sir! Camel spit...spitting. Is that the box of fuses for the entire prison?

DICK BARTON: It certainly is.

CHARLES: I've got an idea, sir. My mother would never forgive me for what I'm about to do, but needs must.

DICK BARTON: I'm way ahead of you, Charles, and it's a corking good idea. — Spit

Enter the gang.

HUGE: So, Barton. No sign of little pussykins yet. I gave you enough time. Your hour is up.

DICK BARTON: And your day has come.

handwritten: This camel's going to spit — massive
handwritten: Snot
handwritten: coughing
handwritten: Sound effects (naturlk)

> *DICK BARTON and CHARLES prepare themselves and spit into the box of death. It explodes madly, causing the place to be plunged into darkness and confusion.*

Well done, Charles. This way!

Music: 'The Devil's Gallop'.

BBC ANNOUNCER: And so the greatest escape begins. With the entire electric system of the prison disabled, Barton and Charles climb up into the laundry room where they consider their options.

Scene 9

The escape.

DICK BARTON: Right. This is the plan. First we escape in this laundry basket. Then we find out who put me in jail and clear my name. Then we turn up in time to foil the Great Plot, whatever it is and then we save the Free World. Sound good to you?

CHARLES: Fine by me.

DICK BARTON: Good man.

CHARLES: By the way, I found this in the Professor's pocket!

DICK BARTON: What do you mean you *found* it in the Professor's pocket?

CHARLES: (*Sheepish.*) Well, you know.

DICK BARTON: Section Three. *Barton never commits an offence in the criminal code, no matter how desirable the means may be argued to justify the end.*

CHARLES: You didn't. I did.

DICK BARTON: Good point. Give it to me.

He does.

Ah good. It's the capsule of chemicals that I need in order to make Dudley the Deadly Duck work.

CHARLES: The what?

— it squirts a foul chemical

DICK BARTON: Look at this. (*He demonstrates.*) Come on, let's go! (*He squirts the duck.*) Good lad, Dudley!

quack

BBC ANNOUNCER: It's chequered flags and champagne showers all round as their stoically sterling steed steadily steers its stash of stowaways towards the next stop, deep in the bowels of His Majesty's Pleasure…

DICK BARTON: Well Charles. By the information my nose is giving me, I'd say we're in a sewer.

CHARLES: Yes, sir. I think you're probably right.

DICK BARTON: Well. Only one thing for it. Best foot forward. Let's try and find a drain.

BBC ANNOUNCER: And it's three cheers for good old penal plumbing as our heroes trudge with transient trepidation towards safety…

DICK BARTON: Fantastic! A drain! And there's grass around the lip. You know what that means? We're outside the prison!

They have a hearty celebration. — *canned applause*

CHARLES: Sir.

DICK BARTON: Yes?

CHARLES: How do we get up there? (*He looks up.*)

DICK BARTON: Ah.

Strange glugging noise. Then running water.

CHARLES: Sir.

DICK BARTON: Yes?

CHARLES: Did you hear that? This doesn't seem all that safe anymore does it.

DICK BARTON: It doesn't, does it. Keep your cool. Things will improve.

The water is running faster.

CHARLES: In fact it seems to be getting deeper.

DICK BARTON: Yes.

CHARLES: And deeper.

The water starts engulfing them.

DICK BARTON: I've noticed.

CHARLES: The level's rising, sir. Sir, I don't think I can…

DICK BARTON: Charles?

CHARLES: Sir! Sir! Where are you, sir?

DICK BARTON: Charles, try and hang on…

CHARLES: Oh Lord, help us please! Sir!

More water.

Where are you…sir?!!!

BBC ANNOUNCER: Disaster! Our hero really is up to his neck in it this time! Will his plucky young sidekick find him in time to haul them both to safety? Will the alarm be raised by now? Have Jock, Snowy and Colonel Gardener really abandoned our hero? Is this real life, or is this just fantasy? What's to become of poor Mrs Horrocks? Who framed Dick Barton? And where's that cup of tea you promised me half an hour ago? All these

67

questions and more will be addressed after the interval, during which I will be probing myself with the all-too-important question: 'Will I be closing the next episode by saying "tune in to the next exciting instalment of...Snowy White, Special Agent!"?'

End of Act One.

ACT TWO

BBC ANNOUNCER: Welcome back to this gripping, epic tale. A tale so complicated that I feel perhaps a detailed recapitulation is required. So. In the first half, Dick Barton was framed, put in prison, and now he's escaped, but only as far as a sewerage pipe, deep in the bowels of Dartmoor. A pipe which, as we left them to go and get a quick pint and an ice-cream, had begun to fill with evil, foul smelling stuff, the name of which I am prevented by BBC guidelines from saying before nine o'clock. Yes, he's up the proverbial creek, without the necessary equipment. But wait! What's that? Luckily for out heroes, Governor Banks has returned from his long lunch and is, to speak proverbially, about to wave an old friend off to the docks! But as he prepares to release another prisoner will he remember his manners and pull the chains of justice?

Scene 1

Sound effect of toilet chain being pulled. DICK BARTON and CHARLES are spewed onto the stage. They brush themselves off. CHARLES is covered in stuff and very wet. DICK BARTON is spotless.

CHARLES: Ah there you are, sir. Thought I'd lost you for a minute. Are you alright?

DICK BARTON: Oh yes. Everything's alright I think, although I'm a bit flushed.

CHARLES: Ha ha! Flushed! Brilliant! Ha ha ha!

DICK BARTON: Why are you laughing?

CHARLES: No reason. Sir. How come you're completely spotless, and what's that smell?

DICK BARTON: It's a perk of the job and it's roses. I always come up smelling that way. Any more questions?

CHARLES: Where are we?

DICK BARTON: We're on Dartmoor. I have to admit I'm a bit disorientated. Might take a while to get the old bearings back... Now. Is that a group of mulberry bushes over there would you say, Charles?

CHARLES: Definitely, sir.

DICK BARTON: In that case, don't go that way.

CHARLES: Why, sir?

DICK BARTON: Unexploded ordnance mines. Left over from the war. Very nasty. Blow us sky high if we step on one of those.

CHARLES: What should we do?

DICK BARTON: Good question. Here's where you learn a little about the art of the Special Agent. You see that couple over there by that oak tree, practising some form of highly vocalised close-contact naked martial art? We'll borrow their discarded clothes and make our way to safety.

CHARLES: Is that a farmhouse over there?

DICK BARTON: Well spotted, young Charles. You're learning fast. Now let's try and commandeer these clothes before we're noticed. What a stroke of luck that they're both gentlemen. Although I have to say those exercises leave a lot to be desired. Must be hell on that poor chap's knees. This way, towards the light.

BBC ANNOUNCER: And so they make their way, in their new clothes, towards the farmhouse where they are given a warm welcome, an offer of a bed and a nightcap. But, his nose weakened by the ordeal in the sewer, our hero fails to notice that the night-cap is drugged. He and Charles fall unconscious and are gagged and bound and sold as slaves to an ambitious Egyptian toothpick magnate, anxious to invest his fortune in farming ventures, who puts our heroes to work on a cotton plantation in the West Midlands. But due to the wrong weather conditions for cotton-growing, the plantation goes bust and they escape, only to be impounded by the Inland Revenue and forced to join a travelling circus which is destroyed by a plague of urchins and they escape. A man with a moustache and a monkey offers them a lift in his zeppelin. But the wind is blowing the wrong way and they end up over the Indian Ocean, where the zeppelin is shot down by fanatically religious pirates, convinced they are witnessing the second coming of the evil flying god known as the Antigherkin. They half-drown for a second time, get picked up by mind-reading dolphins who carry them to a friendly millionaire's boat where they are drugged again, fall unconscious and wake up in a strange foreign land where the natives speak a devilishly difficult language, incomprehensible to us.

Scene 2

A pigeon loft. The sound of nesting pigeons.

DICK BARTON and CHARLES wake up to find a man standing over them.

TAPPY: Way aye man. Are yez ahlreet like? *Alright there lad?*

DICK BARTON: Careful, Charles. I don't know what heathen country we've ended up in but If he asks any questions just give name, rank and number.

CHARLES: Sir. It's alright. I think I know where we are.

DICK BARTON: Where are we?

CHARLES: We're in the North.

DICK BARTON: The what?

CHARLES: The North. It's a place in England.

DICK BARTON: What? We're in England? Then why the devil does that fellow insist on assaulting our ears with that primitive gobbledygook?

CHARLES: That's how they speak here. He's actually speaking a form of English. It's called an accent.

DICK BARTON: Never heard the like.

Enter MACKY, POTTY and BAZ.

POTTY: Well I'll go to the foot of our stotties.

BAZ: Hecky thump! Me too like.

MACKY: Alreet alreet. I's 'll take care o' things from noo on. Tappy, yez can relax. Drink, anyone? (*He holds up a bottle of gin and a bottle of tonic.*)

DICK BARTON: Stop! What do you think you're doing? My friend and I never touch alcohol. It's part of the Special Agent Code. Lucky I stopped him in time, eh Charles?

CHARLES: Yes. Thank you. The last thing I needed after weeks of being locked up in a cell, followed by days without food or comfort, was a cool refreshing gin and tonic.

DICK BARTON: Exactly. It's a rocky road. One minute you're at home with your wife enjoying what seems like a harmless drink, the next you're a tragically pathetic shadow of your true self, frequenting bars, meeting friends and chatting to like-minded people. (*To MACKY.*) Well. Thanks awfully for the hospitality. Most kind and all that, but we'll be off now if you don't mind. Come on, Charles.

MACKY: Relax, Mr Barton. Ye divvunt want tae get oot of here too soon, like.

POTTY: Thy's best off stayin' wi' us like.

TAPPY: Aye. Much safer.

BAZ: We just want tae protect ye like.

MACKY: Well. We'se'll leave thas alone now and go to our bedroom. (*He clicks his fingers.*)

The boys all leave very quickly, excitedly.

Thas'll probably want to rest and recuperate, like. We've plenty to do come tomorrow like. Sleep tight, and take care of thyselves. And remember to watch out for the dangers. (*He exits.*)

DICK BARTON: There's something odd about them.

CHARLES: What do you suppose they meant by 'the dangers'?

BAZ: (*Popping his head in.*) Wolves, wolves, watch out for the deadly wolves! (*He goes.*)

Pause.

(*Pops his head in again.*) And we've got a cat. (*He goes.*)

Pause.

(*Pops his head in again.*) But she doesn't go out because of the wolves.

MACKY: (*Pops his head in – whispers.*) Miles from nowhere, miles from nowhere!

BAZ: Oh yeah, and we're miles from nowhere and ye can't get out coz it's all locked and it's very dangerous and stuff.

DICK BARTON: Just who are you people?

MACKY: Allow me to introduce myself. My name is
Norbert Ham. I have the dubious honour of being the
chairman of your very own fan club, the official one,
mind. We are your greatest fans, Mr Barton, and you are
not going to leave this place until you agree, and believe
me Mr Barton, you will agree, to have your picky taken
with us and sign our books.

DICK BARTON: And then I can go?

MACKY: Erm. Well no, coz you can't get out and there's
the dangers. So you'll have to stay for a little while,
while we sort that out.

TAPPY: We thought maybe if you stayed with us for a
while you could tell us stories at night and maybe write
your memoirs –

POTTY: – and we could help you and be nice to you and –

BAZ: – stroke you and wind you and change your nappy.

They all look at BAZ.

DICK BARTON: So this is what Mother meant by the cost
of fame. And I suppose right here is where I start paying.
Anyone got a pen?

MACKY: Erm…no. I haven't. Potty?

POTTY: No. Don't carry one.

TAPPY: Me neither.

BAZ: Nope.

MACKY: Oh. Well then I'll just have to go out and buy one.

DICK BARTON: In the middle of the night?

MACKY: Well I'll go next door.

DICK BARTON: I thought we were miles from nowhere.

POTTY: We are. We're miles from *nowhere,* but quite close to next door.

MACKY: That's right. I'll be back in a tick.

CHARLES: But you can't go out.

MACKY: Why not?

DICK BARTON: The dangers!

CHARLES: Arooooooooooo!!!!!

MACKY: Oh. Them.

DICK BARTON: So. We're miles from nowhere and we can't go outside. There are four autograph books for me to sign and we've got no pen. What's the plan?

Nobody has one.

Right. If you need something done, do it yourself. *I'll* go next door and get a pen.

MACKY: Wait! How do we know you're going to come back?

DICK BARTON: I'm not. I'm going to escape.

POTTY: But the wolves!

DICK BARTON: There aren't any.

POTTY: Oh you've discovered that one?

DICK BARTON: Thank you. I have now.

The lads admonish POTTY.

Sad music, please, I'm going to depart.

Sad music...

Well. Charlie, old boy, this is where we go our separate ways.

CHARLES: Hmph. Funny.

DICK BARTON: What?

CHARLES: You called me Charlie.

DICK BARTON: So?

CHARLES: Well. It's just…you've never called me that before.

DICK BARTON: What of it?

CHARLES: Nothing. It's just…funny, that's all.

DICK BARTON: Is it?

CHARLES: Erm. Well no, I suppose it's not that funny. Oh well. What now for you?

DICK BARTON: First things first. I have to find out who put me in this situation, give them a thorough seeing-to and clear my name. Then it's time for action. I would take you with me, old bean, but it could get dangerous from here on in. I'm better off doing it alone. Farewell, old friend. And if you ever need anything, just give me a call.

CHARLES: Will do. Goodbye, sir.

DICK BARTON: D'you know, there's something about you, Charlie. Ever since I met you I've thought that. Something very… I don't know. It's something you have that makes you different from other chaps. I wish to God I could put my finger on it.

CHARLES: Me too, sir. Me too.

DICK BARTON salutes.

Goodbye Charlie

DICK BARTON: (*Sings.*)
GOODBYE CHARLIE, I MUST LEAVE YOU
I MUST GO AND CLEAR MY NAME

CHARLES: But Mr Barton, I know you're innocent, I could tell them…

DICK BARTON: (*Sings.*)
YES, BUT NO-ONE WOULD BELIEVE YOU.
(OH THE DREADFUL PRICE OF FAME!)
ONCE SO FULL OF ADMIRATION
NOW THE PUBLIC SPITS AND SNARLS
I'LL RESTORE MY REPUTATION.
GOODBYE, DEAD-EYE CHARLES.

MACKEY/TAPPY: (*Together.*) We've found a pen –

POTTY: It were sitting on the piano keys –

BAZ: So now you can sign our memorabilia!

DICK BARTON: You really are the giddy limit. I haven't time to…

NORTHERNERS: (*Sing.*)
MR BARTON WE'RE GETTING LAIRY
MR BARTON

He bids to escape.

OH NO!
YOU MUST CHANGE YOUR ITINERARY
SIGN OUR SMALL PORTFOLIO

They each produce huge books.

DON'T SIGN IT WILLY NILLY
SIGN EACH PAGE WITH CARE
WE WOULD RATHER YOU DID IT VOLUNTARY
BUT IF NOT – BEWARE!

DICK BARTON: Can you hear yourselves? Can you hear what you're saying? You call yourselves fans of mine – if you were true admirers then you would realise that when my country needs me. *I must go!* And you would certainly not try to detain me with peripheral ephemera.

It's not just the sceptred isle either, it's all the British Dominions, all our beloved pink bits across the globe. What sort of a world do you want? A world in which chaos, anarchy and the forces of darkness prevail and cow us into submission? Or a world where every Briton stands upright and strong against tyranny, and a world where – because of our example – our pink bits stand proud and firm as well! Now, either get out of my way or – if you are the proper fans and the decent follows you claim to be – give me a rousing choral send-off as I stride out to face the untold dangers ahead. What do you say chaps??

NORTHERNERS/CHARLES: (*Sing.*)

MR BARTON, YOU'RE LEGENDARY
OUR HEARTS ARE AGLOW
MAY WE ADD AS A COROLLARY
YOU'RE A HUMAN DYNAMO
HOW COULD WE BE SO SILLY?
WHEN ENGLAND CALLS, YOU'RE THERE
THO' THE THOUGHT'S NOT REVOLUTIONARY –
YOU'RE THE ANSWER TO OUR PRAYER!

Repeat with DICK BARTON singing...

DICK BARTON: (*Sings.*)

GOODBYE CHARLIE I MUST LEAVE YOU
I MUST GO AND CLEAR MY NAME
GOODBYE CHARLIE I MUST LEAVE YOU
IT IS TIME TO 'PLAY THE GAME'
YOU HAVE BEEN A FINE COMPANION
SUCH A LOYAL CHUM IS RARE
BUT, FOR NOW, FAREWELL MY YOUNG D'ARTAGNON
I MUST ANSWER TO A PRAYER.

BBC ANNOUNCER: I don't know about you, but I feel after that stirring melody our cockles are as warm as toast. Back on Dartmoor, a place still littered with the debris of war, our friend the Professor has managed to run away from his colleagues, and now, fearing for his own safety, is desperate to get in touch with Dick Barton. Stay away from the mulberry bushes, Professor Pete.

Scene 3

Dartmoor.

PETER is in the rain, with his mobile telephone. He looks around to make sure he's safe. He takes out a note.

PETER: Ah, this seems as good a place as any to read the note that Dick Barton gave me and told me to read in a private moment just before his foiled execution in the prison. *Dear Professor Peter. Just to say two things. Firstly, thanks for trying to help. And secondly, I forgive you for what you are about to do, I only hope God will too. Yours, Dick Barton.* What can that mean? Forgive me for what I'm about to do? I must try and call him… Hello?… Hello? Operator? Can you put me through to Mr Dick Barton?

LAUGHING JAKE and LATE BOB have snuck up behind him.

I need to get an urgent message to him. Yes. It reads…

JAKE: Hello Peter.

PETER: Er…hello Jake, hello Bob…yes…it reads: 'You scum. You enemy of my boss. I kill you.' Thanks. Hello lads. You lost too?

JAKE: (*Laughs heartily.*) No.

BOB: Trying to get through to your lover boy, eh Peter?

PETER: I don't know what you mean.

JAKE: Your best boy, old Dicky.

PETER: What, me? Friends with Barton? Don't be daft. We're sworn enemies.

BOB: You sure?

PETER: Oh yes of course.

Sound effect of a cock crowing.

JAKE: Three denials eh, Peter? That's good enough for me. I believe him. What about you, Bob?

BOB: Oh yes Jake. Most convincing.

JAKE: You're a very lucky man, Peter.

PETER: I… I don't understand. Why am I lucky?

JAKE and BOB get blades out.

JAKE: Usually we use blunted ones.

PETER: But…oh now come on, lads. Don't kill me. Eh? Eh?

BOB: Don't be daft. We're not gonna kill you, you silly old goat. We're just havin' a laugh with ya.

PETER: Oh. Oh, I see. Haha.

JAKE: Nah. We're your mates, remember? It's Barton we're after. And we're going to get him.

PETER: Oh. Great.

BOB: Oh yeah. We know exactly where he is, don't you worry. We're just gonna make sure you take a nice walk and don't come back.

PETER: Oh thanks lads! I appreciate this. I'll send you something from abroad, anonymous like, so no-one suspects you or anything. Oh, thanks lads.

BOB: Come on then, off we go. You're really going places y'know.

PETER: Am I? You got something lined up for me?

JAKE: Oh yeah. You're going far and wide.

BOB: And very very high. 'Here we go round the mulberry bush, the mulberry bush, the mulberry bush…'

BOB/JAKE: 'Here we go round the mulberry bush…'

PETER: 'On a cold and frosty morning.'

They laugh heartily…boom!!!

BBC ANNOUNCER: A chilling warning to anybody who tries to foil this particular plot. Watch out, Dick! Imagine the fear that courses through our hero's veins as he sets off on a personal crusade against his faceless enemy, unaware of where or who, the why the what and how of it. Blind and mapless in uncharted territory. Almost any means of transport will do…

Scene 4

A Haywain.

Sound effect of horse plodding along very very very slowly indeed

NATHANIEL: Whoa there, Bessy!

JEDAKAIAH: Here, Nathaniel. You hear a rustlin' sound in the back of thy haywain?

NATHANIEL: Th'art right, Jedakaiah my companion. More'n likely that'll be a mysterious stranger having a bit of a scuffle with himself.

JEDAKAIAH: Can you still get arrested for that?

NATHANIEL: Depends whether you count a haywain as a public place.

DICK BARTON pops his head up.

DICK BARTON: Evening.

81

NATHANIEL: No, by the look of him I'd say he'll get away with a fine and a job at the Palace. Can we help, stranger?

DICK BARTON: I'm afraid I'm going to have to requisition this haywain on behalf of the British government…in a roundabout sort of way.

NATHANIEL: Requisition?

DICK BARTON: Yes. I suppose you could call it a hayjack.

BBC ANNOUNCER: That joke is currently appearing as the lame donkey in Mrs Nethergill's Old Time Pantomime at the Frensham and Frimley Ladies' Guild.

DICK BARTON: Sorry about that. Now please relinquish control of your haywain. This is a matter of national importance.

JEDAKAIAH: You're in a bit of a hurry if you ask me.

DICK BARTON: I didn't ask you. Is that a copy of the Radio Times?

JEDAKAIAH: Some say it be. And so, if It be that, so it be.

DICK BARTON: Could I possibly borrow it for a moment?

JEDAKAIAH: Oh no. That would mean trusting you to give it back. Nobody trusts anybody else any more since that Barton fella fell by the wayside.

DICK BARTON: I see. Then I wonder if you could do me a small favour. Could you read me what it says under 6:45 on the Light Programme?

JEDAKAIAH: Reckon I could.

Pause.

DICK BARTON: Good. Then please…please please please!

JEDAKAIAH: Alright. Let me have a look now. Right, here we are.

6:45. Dick Barton, Special Agent.

Pause.

DICK BARTON: Yes I've got that bit. Read on read on!

JEDAKAIAH: Let me see now… Our fallen hero visits Snowy…and…

DICK BARTON: Yes yes yes…! Oh please! How much more of this must I endure?!

NATHANIEL: By my reckonin' about another five scenes.

DICK BARTON: Come on, come on! He visits Snowy AND…??!!!

JEDAKAIAH: …discovers an important truth.

DICK BARTON: An important truth. At last. Snowy. So that's it. I've got to get to Snowy. To the nearest train station please! And don't spare the horses! Although, by the look of this one, perhaps you'd better.

JEDAKAIAH: Why you off to the train station then? To catch a train I shouldn't wonder.

NATHANIEL: More'n likely I reckon.

DICK BARTON: Didn't you read what it said in there? I've got to find out an important truth.

JEDAKAIAH: What important truth's that then?

DICK BARTON: I won't know til I get there.

JEDAKAIAH: Well you'd best hurry up then.

DICK BARTON: That's the general idea. Doesn't this thing go any faster?

NATHANIEL: Oh no. We're exceeding the speed limit as it is.

DICK BARTON: I see.

NATHANIEL: You'd be best off walking if truth be known. Old Bessy's on her last legs. Liable to drop dead any minute. D'you know I had that George Formby in the back of my haywain once. Now he's a genius.

JEDAKAIAH: Reckon you be talkin' to yerself, Nathaniel. Young fella's got out and walked.

NATHANIEL: Sensible really.

JEDAKAIAH: Why's that then?

Sound effect of horse neighing, coughing, and then collapsing.

JEDAKAIAH: I see. What we need's a bit of help. Are you a member of the Hay Hay?

NATHANIEL: Nope.

JEDAKAIAH: What you gonna do with yer dead horse then?

NATHANIEL: Don't know. Flog it, probably.

BBC ANNOUNCER: (*Off.*) Yes, I suggest you do that. (*On.*) Ladies and gentlemen, we have a slight technical hitch. Due to a change of staff there appears to have been a breakdown in communications between the link-writing department and myself. I can only apologise and erm (*Looking around.*) ...entertain you with (*He finds a book.*) ...some words from my dictionary. 'Anophelosis', a morbid state caused by extreme frustration, 'Hemothymia', an irresistible desire to murder, and 'Pygalgia', an excruciating pain in the buttocks... (*Off.*) Yes, I'm talking about you. (*On.*) Meanwhile, back on the road...

Scene 5

Fortune Teller Song

DICK BARTON: Excuse me, could you tell me the way to…

GYPSY: (*Sings.*)
CROSS MY PALM WITH SILVER, MY DEAR,
THEN I'LL REVEAL THE SECRETS YOU LONG TO HEAR

DICK BARTON: Madam, I really…

GYPSY: (*Sings.*)
CROSS MY PALM!!

DICK BARTON: (*Sings.*)
I CAN'T, I'M BROKE

GYPSY: (*Sings.*)
AW. NEVER MIND, I'LL LET YOU HAVE A READING ON ACCOUNT –
YOU SEEM LIKE A DECENT BLOKE

DICK BARTON: Yes, but I just –

GYPSY: (*Sings.*)
NEPTUNE'S IN ASCENDANCE WITH MARS,
VIRGO IS RISING – EV'RYTHING IS IN THE STARS

DICK BARTON: Oh, really!

GYPSY: (*Sings.*)
MERCURY'S UP – THE FATES ARE ALIGNED

You are such a typical Libra.

DICK BARTON: Taurus, I think you'll find

GYPSY: I knew it. (*Sings.*)

CAPRICORN AND VENUS ARE IN CONJUNCTION
PLUTO ENTERS PISCES AT AN ASTRAL FUNCTION
I WAS GIFTED BY ARIES WITH SECOND SIGHT!

OH! YOUR RISING SIGNS ARE JUST DYNAMITE!
ONE, TWO, THREE –
'YOU GOT THE SUN IN URANUS, AND THE MOON…'

DICK BARTON: Yes, quite.

GYPSY: (*Sings.*)

DON'T EXCITE YOURSELF, YOU MUST STAY CALM
LET ME DO A READING OF YOUR PALM
ALL THE THINGS THE SPHERES MAY HAVE PLANNED
ARE WRITTEN IN THE LINES UPON YOUR HAND

FIRST THE LIFE-LINE IS
CONNECTED TO THE FATE-LINE
THEN THE FATE-LINE'S
CONNECTED TO THE HEART-LINE
SO THE HEART-LINE'S
CONNECTED TO THE HEAD-LINE
THE HEAD-LINE'S CONNECTED TO THE FATE LINE
'SO HEAR THE WORD OF THE LORD'

DICK BARTON: All I want to know is…

GYPSY: (*Sings.*)

MONDAY: FINANCE SEEMS ON THE MEND
TUESDAY: AVOID ARGUING WITH A FRIEND
WEDNESDAY:

DICK BARTON: Could we stick to today?

GYPSY: (*Sings.*)

OOH. YOU ARE IMPATIENT!
IF THAT'S WHAT YOU WANT, OKAY.

DICK BARTON: (*Sings.*)

HOORAY!

GYPSY: (*Sings.*)

I SEE FIVE – NO, TEN THOUSAND POUNDS ON YOUR HEAD
THAT'S TEN THOUSAND CAPTURED – ALIVE OR DEAD
A COCKNEY EX-SIDEKICK IS HAPPY DOING YOUR JOB OH!

And about two hundred and thirty yards behind that old barn, baying for your blood, and extremely heavily armed…

IS AN INCREDIBLY ANGRY MOB

DICK BARTON: Thank you. And the way to the station?

GYPSY: That way.

DICK BARTON: Obliged! (*Exits.*)

GYPSY: They fall for it everytime. Load of old rubbish if you ask me.

BBC ANNOUNCER: And so our hero bounds towards the station, desperate to catch the last train out of there. Over, he leaps, to platform twelve where the mighty black engine awaits, steaming, pumping, tooting, balham and collier's wood. Just in time, he dives into a carriage. First class, of course.

Scene 6

A train carriage.

DICK BARTON enters. A beautiful Audrey Hepburn type is enjoying a cigarette and a glass of champagne.

DICK BARTON: Phew! Just in time. A moment later and all would have been lost. Mind if I sit here?

She says nothing, but blows smoke in his face.

Charmed, I'm sure. Why aren't we moving?

TANNOY: *We apologise for the late running of the last train out of here. This is due to our inability to perform even the simplest of tasks. The next stop for this train will be the one just a bit further down the track, where this train will terminate and passengers can get a special horse and carriage service to a destination not really close enough to the one you*

WISBEY / BEDNARCZYK / CRAIG

wanted. I would like to inform passengers that there is a buffet service on this train, which will open just before you get off and will remain poorly stocked for the rest of the journey. Once again we would like to apologise for the inconvenience caused to your journey, but there is currently nobody available who can be bothered to do it.

DENNIS, VERA's husband, returns from the toilet.

DICK BARTON: Excuse me, sir. Did you hear that?

VERA: Disgusting it is. It's a naffin' disgrace. The whole country's gone to pot since Dick Barton disappeared. Transport's all wrong, isn't it, dear? The King still refuses to get out of bed. And George Formby's given up the ukelele.

DICK BARTON: So it's not all bad then.

VERA: Oh yes it is. No-one trusts nobody. My husband don't like it, I don't mind telling you. I said, you don't like it, do you dear? It's all since the fall of… (*Sniff, sniff.*) dear Mr Barton.

I wonder what he's doing now that he's escaped from prison. It's such a shame he went to the bad.

DICK BARTON: Went to the bad? But he was innocent. He was wrongly imprisoned.

VERA: Oh, we know that. It was inside that he went bad, apparently.

DENNIS: He felt betrayed, you see. One day all was well. Like a guardian angel he was, looking over us all.

VERA: Then he fell from grace, the malevolent maggot of vengeance grew within him, and he turned to evil.

DENNIS: Such a bright star he was. And now he's escaped and he wants to turn Britain into his own hell on earth!

VERA: Hell on Earth! Murder us in our beds, he will!

DENNIS: He's evil, and everybody's terrified of him!

VERA: The new Prince of Darkness, he is!

DICK BARTON: Surely you don't believe that?

VERA: It's true.

DENNIS: Prophesied, it is.

VERA: On the wireless, every day.

DICK BARTON: By whom?

DENNIS: The Voice.

DICK BARTON: The what?

VERA: The Master. He speaks to the nation when the pips are on.

DENNIS: Speaks the truth he does.

DICK BARTON: The truth eh? Or his version of it. As Snowy would say, I've been proper goosed by propaganda. Well, I've got a proposition for you. What would you do if I proved to you that the Voice is wrong, and I made Barton appear before your very eyes, in the flesh?

VERA: Ooh, the flesh. Oooooh Dick Barton, in the flesh. Ooooh the flesh.

DENNIS: A vision!

DICK BARTON: Well?

VERA: Ooooh, I should lie on the floor and frustrate meself in front of 'im.

DICK BARTON: Don't you mean you'd *pro*strate yourself in front of him?

VERA: You have your fantasy and I'll have mine.

DICK BARTON: Then prepare to be frustrated. I shall prove to you that Dick Barton is good.

VERA: How?

DICK BARTON produces a bunch of flowers and takes off his hat.

DICK BARTON: Madam, I am Dick Barton.

VERA: Ooh look, dear. Flowers! What a gentleman!

DENNIS: And he's tooken his hat off in front of a lady.

VERA: Dick Barton. It really is you.

DENNIS: The real thing.

VERA: In the flesh.

DENNIS: What do we do now?

VERA: Well, we ought to help him in his adventure.

DENNIS: Help save the free world.

Pause.

VERA/DENNIS: (*Together.*) Ten thousand quid though. Get him!!! (*They both pounce on him.*)

BBC ANNOUNCER: Oh the pain of it! Our hero's in real trouble. But where, oh where, is Mr Huge during all this? Not far behind him, I fear!

Scene 7

Vendetta Song

MR HUGE: (*Sings.*)
I WILL KILL YOU. I WILL BREAK YOU
AS YOUR COMRADES ALL FORSAKE YOU
I WILL KILL AND 'UNDERTAKE' YOU

He is pleased with this rhyme.

I SHALL MAKE YOU SUICIDAL
I SHALL SMASH THIS FALLEN IDOL
I SHALL HAVE YOU…CRUCIFIED…

He is less pleased with this one.

YOU HAVE DARE TO DISOBEY ME
YOU WILL FIND THOSE WHO BETRAY ME
MUST EVENTUALLY REPAY ME
YOU'VE NOT WON, DEAR BARTON; AU CONTRAIRE
THIS IS WAR, DEAR BARTON – C'EST LA GUERRE
I WILL CRUSH YOU – SO BEWARE.

WHEN YOU'RE MEETING PEOPLE LOOK INTO THEIR FACES –
EVEN IF YOU THINK YOU KNOW THEM –
I HAVE PEOPLE IN THE HIGHEST OF HIGH PLACES
I HAVE EVEN MORE BELOW THEM.
WHEN AT LAST YOU THINK YOU'VE FOUND A DEVOTEE
YOU WILL FIND THAT HE IS ANSWERABLE TO ME!
THERE HAS NEVER BEEN A BETTER
MORE ENJOYABLE VENDETTA.
YOU MAY THINK YOU'VE ESCAPED ME,
BUT BE CAREFUL HOW YOU TREAD
FOR I SWEAR I'LL HAVE VENGEANCE,
I'LL NOT REST UNTIL YOU'RE DEAD.

BBC ANNOUNCER: Look out, Dick! He's coming to get you! Once again our hero finds himself lost on the Moors. This time, the Yorkshire Moors…

Scene 8

The Moors.

DICK BARTON: Well. Here I am again. Exhausted and sweating profusely on top of a dangerous moor. I feel like Desdemona. I don't know why I said that. I don't even get it. Oh, for some semblance of sleep. To sleep, perchance to sleep a bit more. And food. I'm so hungry. But most of all, a raging thirst. A desperation for just one drop of the great giver of life. The very God-given element that makes up seventy percent of an Englishman's body. Tea. Oh, what would I not give for some tea. A cup of Tea! A cup of Tea! My Kingdom for…!

GORKY: Cup of tea! Cup of tea!

DICK BARTON: Great Scott, there's an echo.

GORKY: Sorry to sneak up on you like that, sir. I'm a wandering cup-of-tea salesman and business is very slow on the Moors tonight. Could you force yourself to partake of a humble drop?

DICK BARTON: Oh please, please yes! You life saver! Now. I've got no money I'm afraid, but I'm desperate. I'll do anything to repay you. Just name it.

GORKY: Well, actually there are three things you could do for me, but we'll talk about that after your cup of tea.

DICK BARTON: Tea! You saviour, I could kiss you!

GORKY: That's the first thing.

DICK BARTON: Tell me, my fine friend, what sort of tea do you have?

GORKY: Well I do happen to have a freshly brewed pot of Earl Grey.

DICK BARTON: Earl Grey! Earl Grey, you genius! Oh, thankyou thankyou thankyou! I'm on my knees in gratitude! If there's anything I can do to repay you!

GORKY: That was the second thing. It does get very lonely up here sir. And I am partial…

DICK BARTON: Pour the tea.

GORKY: No need to be curt. Now, as company policy I have to ask, will you be having your tea here or taking it away with you?

DICK BARTON: Oh. Here, please.

GORKY: And would you like it tall, grande, venti, fatti, biggi, smalli, widey, roundy, nasty or smelly?

DICK BARTON: What?

GORKY: And would you like me to make it with milk, steamed milk, boiled milk, deep-fried milk, goat's milk, lemon, cinnamon, honey, or lard? Alternatively, sir might prefer the please just shut up and give me a cup of tea before I kill you option.

DICK BARTON: Yes. That one.

GORKY: Right you are, sir. Sir might also be interested to know I am currently selling a range of totally unsatisfying but highly expensive stale Italian biscuits.

DICK BARTON: Sir will make do with the tea. Thank you so much. Oh come to me my little darling. Not you! Ah. Tea. Lovely, hot… Wait a minute. This isn't Earl Grey. This is Lapsang Souchong. Only a foreigner would mistake Lapsang Souchong for Earl Grey. Alright, you. Who are you working for?

GORKY: Don't hit me! Don't hit me!

DICK BARTON: What have you got in yer bag? Come on, Let's have a feel.

GORKY: That was the third thing.

DICK BARTON: You'll give me that bag, sir, or you'll feel the back of my hand.

GORKY: Ooh, four!

DICK BARTON: The bag, please. Hmm. Some sort of leather studded torture equipment, eh? I see your game. Oh, and a large, India rubber thing shaped like a… actually I've never seen one of those before. What is it?

GORKY: It's a cosh.

DICK BARTON: So. You were going to knock me out and then torture me, eh?

GORKY: No, those things are for my own private use, sir.

DICK BARTON: Silence!

GORKY: I only wanted to have a little fun.

DICK BARTON: You've got exactly fifteen seconds, by which time I expect to have received a full confession. I will have satisfaction.

GORKY: Five! Alright alright! Don't hit me. I'll confess everything. But first, have pity, sir. I'm actually a lady in disguise, fallen on hard times.

DICK BARTON: Oh, my dear! I'm so terribly sorry. I had no idea.

GORKY: Would you mind awfully turning round while I adjust the seam of my stockings?

DICK BARTON: Not at all, my dear. With pleasure.

GORKY: Thank you. I thought a gentleman was supposed to always remove his hat in front of a lady.

DICK BARTON: Oh of course. How thoughtless of me.

GORKY: You Englishmen make my job so easy. (*He coshes him over the head.*)

Lights out.

The lights come back up, focussed very sharply on DICK BARTON. It is as if he is being interrogated.

VOICE: Barton. Barton.

DICK BARTON: Who are you? Where am I?

VOICE: This is the voice of God.

DICK BARTON: Is this a dream?

VOICE: Probably.

DICK BARTON: What do you want?

VOICE: Beware, Barton. Everything will be alright as long as you stay away from the moors.

DICK BARTON: I'm on the moors.

VOICE: (*Off.*) He says he's on the moors. What? Alright, keep yer thorns on. (*To DICK BARTON.*) Well don't go on any more.

DICK BARTON: I told you, I'm on a moor.

VOICE: No, I mean don't go on any more moors.

DICK BARTON: Right. Is that everything?

VOICE: Think so, yes.

DICK BARTON: Right. Thanks.

VOICE: Not a problem.

BBC ANNOUNCER: And so, as our hero falls unconscious for the umpteenth time, we cross over to the former Barton office at Wimpole Street where something very mysterious is happening.

Scene 9

DICK BARTON's office.

COLONEL GARDENER and MRS HORROCKS.

COLONEL GARDENER: But the most important thing about it is this…and you must commit this to memory…

Enter a 'Carry-On' NURSE, giggling.

(*Suddenly changing the mood.*) And when I woke up
I found I suddenly had three. Is that the time? I'd better
be off, Mrs H. I'll see myself out. I know you can't get
up or speak in any way. Well, nurse. We've done our
business.

NURSE giggles.

I've grasped both matters firmly in hand…

NURSE giggles.

…and probed deeply into it…

NURSE giggles.

…and I think it's time for me to get back on the job…

NURSE giggles.

Is there something up?

NURSE giggles.

How bizarre. I shall take my leave of you. Do take care
of yourselves. And each other. Goodnight. (*He leaves.*)

NURSE: Now, Mrs H. You must be very tired after all that
excitement. Time for beddy night-nights for you, you
naughty girl. I'm sure old cuddlebumps will be back
again. I dunno, you are a caution, havin' a boyfriend at
your age. You're a naughty girl aren't you? Eh? Who's a
naughty naughty girl? Eh? Eh? Who's a naughty naughty
girl?

MRS HORROCKS: Piss off.

*The NURSE storms off, switching the light off, leaving MRS
HORROCKS alone in the darkness. We see her get out of
her bathchair, spooky music, she goes to the desk and rattles
the drawers. She gets something out of the top drawer. Then
she picks up the phone.*

BBC ANNOUNCER: Oh dear, what's going on there? Simultaneously, in a dark, spooky warehouse, our hero finds himself in a bit of a pickle again as he comes round from his stupor to find that he has been not only asleep but unconscious too.

Scene 10

A converted warehouse.

DICK BARTON is tied up in torture gear and strapped to some kind of wheel of torture.

DICK BARTON: Where am I? Am I still dreaming? And why am I dressed like a German? I feel like the Cabaret at a Mediaeval Bar Mitzvah. Hello? No answer. Mind you, I didn't give much time for one. I'll try again.

Enter GORKY.

Ah, no need.

GORKY: (*Stares at him.*) Morning darling. Feeling a little rough?

DICK BARTON: Who the devil are you and where's that cup of tea you promised me? Ow, my head. Where the Dickens am I? It all seems somehow familiar.

GORKY: You're in a converted warehouse, south of London…on the Brighton line

DICK BARTON: The line is immaterial. Wait. Why did I say that? Makes no sense. But I'm sure I've heard it before. Can't wait to get to the bottom of this so I can get back to saying things I understand.

GORKY: You can rant and rave all you like. Soon the Master will be here and all will be revealed.

DICK BARTON: Well tell him to hurry up.

STRANGER: (*From the shadows.*) Alright, Gorky. Leave Mr Barton alone. Get back to your business. I'll take care of things from here.

GORKY: Yes, Master! Anything you say, Master!

STRANGER: Good Gorky. So, Mr Barton. We meet again.

DICK BARTON: Wha…who are you? Show yerself!

He does. It's SNOWY.

Snowy!

SNOWY: Sorry about all this, guv. It was the only way I could get you here without arousing suspicion. Everyone's after you, you see.

DICK BARTON: So what's with Igor here?

GORKY: Gorky!

DICK BARTON: Whatever.

SNOWY: Oh him? He's my sidekick. I hired him from a sidekicks agency.

DICK BARTON: Why on earth did you get an evil foreign one? What's wrong with a decent British model?

SNOWY: Can't get them for love nor money at the moment. They're all tied up in the Ealing comedies. He was all they had left. He's only mock foreign anyway. Bad Gorky! I told you to make Mr Barton feel at home. Is this how you usually treat your guests? Don't answer that. Now release Mr Barton.

DICK BARTON: Thanks. So. Snowy. Your news.

SNOWY: How did you know I had news?

DICK BARTON: Radio Times. Come on, old boy. Let's have it.

SNOWY: Well. Ever since you got done, I've done my bestest to get you undone. I've had me best men on the job. I even had a spy in Prison who sent me letters every day.

DICK BARTON: Ah. That explains the letters to Wimpole St. Carry on.

SNOWY: It was my spy what sent you the dangerous rubber duck. I trust it worked?

DICK BARTON: Oh yes. So. What's the news?

SNOWY: Well. I've discovered that someone somewhere…is plotting to do something sometime possibly soon.

Pause.

DICK BARTON: We might need a little more than that to go on but it's a start. Anything else?

SNOWY: Well. After you escaped, Mr Huge and his henchmen took advantage of the diversion and escaped themselves. Apparently Mr Huge has managed, in disguise, to wangle himself a high powered job that could mean danger for us.

DICK BARTON: I see. Let's think. What job could a criminal mastermind with an Oscar Wilde fix…wait a minute. Brighton Line. The line is immaterial. By George I think I may have it. Gorky.

GORKY: Yes.

DICK BARTON: I want you to drop that bottle.

GORKY: What?

He hasn't got a bottle.

DICK BARTON: Just drop it.

GORKY: Okay.

He pretends to drop it. Sound effect of dustbin lid being dropped, rolling along and finishing with a clang, then a cat meowing.

DICK BARTON: Now I'm going to shoot you with this shotgun.

Sound effect of a doorbell.

Just as I thought. Huge's men have infiltrated the Sound Effects department at Broadcasting House. So that explains the letters to the BBC. Try and wrong-foot me, would you. We'll see about that! Snowy, we've very little time to lose. Do we know the identity of Huge's number two?

SNOWY: Not yet, although I have my suspicions.

DICK BARTON: I've got an idea. Gorky, are you a member of the Sidekick's Union?

GORKY: Oh yes sir, fully paid.

DICK BARTON: And you belong to the Agency? Surely sidekicks must talk to each other. Have you heard anything?

GORKY: Not really, sir. Although the other day I did hear a man mention the words 'Big' and 'Day' in connection with August the thirty first.

DICK BARTON: August the thirty first. What's so special about that day? Who gave you that information?

GORKY: I can't remember, sir. I never caught his name. All I know is he used to be a sidekick and he's Scottish.

DICK BARTON: Scottish and used to be a sidekick? I think we have our culprit, eh Snowy? I think it's about time we paid our Scottish friend a little visit. Snowy. Mac.

SNOWY and GORKY dress DICK BARTON in the mac.

Hat.

They give him the hat.

Send out a message to the criminal world.

Music sting – lighting change – big moment.

Barton's back. And this time, he gets the girl! (*He puts on the hat.*)

SNOWY: What girl's that, guv?

DICK BARTON: Doesn't matter, doesn't matter, it's just an expression.

SNOWY: I'm glad you're back, guv. I never liked being a Special Agent. I only took the job to help get you out of Prison. I'm much happier being a sidekick.

The Sidekick Song

SNOWY: (*Sings.*)
YOU'D THINK A SIDEKICK'S JOB WOULD BE TOO AWFUL
TO CONTEMPLATE, BUT LISTEN, MATE:
TO HAVE A BOSS WHOSE FIGHT WITH THE UNLAWFUL
YOU EMULATE IS REALLY GREAT
A MAN WHO'S ALWAYS SUCH AN INSPIRATION,
WHO SEES IT THROUGH, IS THERE FOR YOU
WHAT'S MORE, THRU' ALL HIS SERVICE TO THE NATION
– I'M AT HIS SIDE
(*Spoken.*) Talk about pride!

SIDEKICK, SIDEKICK, EV'RY YOUNG BOY'S DREAM
SIDEKICK, SIDEKICK, MEMBER OF A TEAM
AND WHEN THE VILLAINS COME TO CALL
IT'S ALL FOR ONE AND ONE FOR ALL!

Repeat.

Dance break.

GORKY joins in.

SNOWY: Gorky, you're fired.

GORKY: Oh well. It was a good job while it lasted.

DICK BARTON: (*Sings.*)
> IT'S TRUE, WHEN SOLVING CRIME I DO IT MY WAY
> – BUT TO MAKE FREE WITH SIMILE
> WE'RE TOLD THAT EVEN CRUSOE HAD HIS FRIDAY,
> AND SO WITH ME BECAUSE YOU SEE
> WITH WATSON, SANCHO PANZA – YES AND TONTO,
> THE FOOL AND LEAR, THE PATTERN'S CLEAR
> IF YOU NEED SOMETHING DONE – AND DOING PRONTO,
> TAKE IT FROM DICK, THIS IS THE TRICK:

DICK BARTON/SNOWY: (*Sing.*)
> GUV'NOR, SIDEKICK – THAT'LL WIN THE RACE
> GUV'NOR, SIDEKICK – EACH MAN IN HIS PLACE
> AND WHEN THE VILLAINS COME TO CALL
> IT'S ALL FOR ONE AND ONE FOR ALL!
> IT'S A MANLY BRAWL – IT'S ALL FOR ONE AND ONE FOR ALL

Repeat.

BBC ANNOUNCER: Full speed ahead to Scotland goes our hero to face his newest nemesis, evil ex-sidekick Jock Anderson. Even as he boards the Barton Bentley with his new sidekick, ex-sidekick-turned-sidekick, Snowy White, the nation's saviour is perplexed, bewildered and not a little miffed by his Caledonian counterpart's defection into the arms of The Ungoodly One.

Scene 11

JOCK's office.

JOCK and KENNY arrive back from a job. KENNY is bursting with pride at being so lucky as to be working with such a hero as JOCK.

KENNY: Och och och och och! Ochity ochity och och och! I love being a Policeman! I'm so excited I might just have another toffee! D'you think I should, sir? Do ya? Do ya? Do ya?

JOCK: Steady on, young Kenny. That'll be your third today.

KENNY: I know but I'm so excited! You were amazing! I can't believe how amazing you were! So brave! And just in the nick of time!

JOCK: Yes. If I'd been a moment later the cat might have gone further up the tree.

KENNY: Oh you saved his wee life, sir! Saved him you did! Can I fill out the form, sir? Can I can I can I please please please please please?!!!

JOCK: If it makes your life worthwhile I've no compunction to stop ye.

KENNY: Oh, thank you thank you thank you sir! You never know, sir. Tomorrow we may even crack the case of the stolen glove.

JOCK: Allegedly, Kenny, allegedly. We don't know if it was stolen. She may have left it on the bus.

KENNY: Och it's so exciting.

JOCK: Yes. I haven't felt this excited since the time I thought my hat had blown off but it hadn't.

The telephone rings.

Hello? Yes? I see. We'll get on to it straight away. Kenny, there's been another double toe-stubbing incident in the Auchentorlie Road. You'd better go down and club them both to death.

KENNY: You don't mean that, sir?

JOCK: Och no. Heat of the moment. Thinking out loud and all that.

KENNY: Och that's alright then.

JOCK: Off ye go then before I scutch yer neep off wi' a ruch-spun haggis. (*Scots Lit. 'Cut your head off with a blunted haggis'.*)

KENNY: Aye, sir. (*Exits.*)

JOCK: Och I dinnae like what this job's turning me into. I'm getting crabbit and crankie and a wee bit snell. I miss the excitement and I've already drifted back into disused dialect. Ah, for the auld days. Memories, eh? Memories... (*He begins a song: 'When I was a Boy...'*)

DICK BARTON: (*Bursts in and interrupts.*) Just in the nick of time!

JOCK: DB!

KENNY: I couldnae stop them, sir!

DICK BARTON: Ever seen a ghost before? Meet your own personal Banquo. Weren't expecting this, eh? So what are you going to do now?

Pause.

KENNY: Would anybody like a cup of tea?

BARTON/SNOWY/JOCK: (*Together.*) Two sugars / Yes please / Aye, nae sugar.

KENNY: Coming up. (*He exits.*)

JOCK: So, what's the plan?

DICK BARTON: You tell me, my dram-guzzling ginger nemesis. You're the one who wanted me out of the way so you could control things from up here.

JOCK: Och not at all! All I wanted was an easy life for
  Daphne. She's at haem noo, ironing my socks and
  recuperating after her recuperative trip awa. I'm getting
  Kenny to take her some of Granny McNair's shortbread
  when he's finished here.

DICK BARTON: Who's Kenny?

JOCK: Och he's my new sidekick. Got him from an agency.

KENNY: (*Re-enters.*) Tea!

DICK BARTON: Wait a minute! Kenny! Do you know
  someone called... Gorky, is it?

KENNY: Gorky. Gorky... Gorky... Gorky. What's his full
  name?

SNOWY: Gorky Hamilton-Smythe.

KENNY: Och, Gorkers Hammers Smythe! Aye. He was in
  my year at Sidekick School. We were on the Evil Course
  together, although I couldnae get any work 'cause my
  face is too bonny so I turned to good instead. I havenae
  seen him for a while. I'm still friends with some of my
  lot. Most of them are in Prison now. My best pal's
  working as a sidekick for a guy called Mr Huge. He
  writes to me every day, although I've no heard from him
  for a wee while.

DICK BARTON: So that explains the letters to Scotland.
  Sorry I doubted you, Jock.

JOCK: Nae bother.

SNOWY: 'Ere, what about me?

DICK BARTON: Oh alright. I'm sorry I doubted you too.
  Kenny, do you have any of those letters to hand?

KENNY: You might be in luck there. Oh no, hang on. I've
  burned them all. Although I do have one in my pocket

that he asked me specifically to send on to the great
Dick Barton if I could find out where he's hiding.

DICK BARTON: So why the devil didn't you?

KENNY: Well I've written to him several times before,
asking for autographs and stuff but he never replied so I
didnae bother.

DICK BARTON: Give it to me.

KENNY: But what about Dick Barton?

DICK BARTON: You're looking at him.

KENNY faints.

DICK BARTON: Let's have a look now. According to this,
Mr Huge gets his daily reports from his number two
who calls him from a telephone box in Soho at midnight
every day. Snowy, could you pull a favour from our
friends at Scotland Yard?

SNOWY: Don't see why not.

DICK BARTON: Good chap. Tell them not to let anybody
near this telephone box between half-past eleven and
half-past twelve tomorrow. Apart from us of course.
Only one question remains. What's so significant about
August the thirty-first?

JOCK: Ah, the big night.

DICK BARTON: So you do know about it?

JOCK: Of course. I listen to it every year. Land of Hope
and Glory, Jerusalem, all the old favourites performed in
the grandeur of the Royal Albert Hall. It's going to be a
special one this year. The King is even getting out of bed
to go along as guest of honour.

DICK BARTON: Of course! How did I miss that one? The Last Night of the Proms! So that's why they've taken control of the BBC.

JOCK: How d'ye ken they've taken control of the BBC?

DICK BARTON: Snowy. Would you like to, or shall I?

SNOWY: All yours, guv.

DICK BARTON: Look, a cow!

Sound effect of duck.

An elephant!

Sound effect of a cow.

JOCK: A long-haired Schnauser goose in leather clogs carrying as motorcycle up a ladder made of cheese.

DICK BARTON: Don't push your luck. Are you with me, lads?

JOCK: Och aye the noo!

SNOWY: Cor blimey, guv!

DICK BARTON: At last, the old team are back together…

Sidekick Song (Reprise)

JOCK: (*Sings.*)
BY JINGS! I MUST ADMIT THAT I'M EXCITED
– I SUPPOSE IT SHOWS!
WE'LL TRADE SOME BLOWS!
IT'S GRAND TO SEE THE TEAM ALL RE-UNITED

SNOWY: Good on yer, ''aggis'.

JOCK: (*Sings.*)
THE BANTER FLOWS
WE'LL FIGHT THE FOES!

SNOWY: (*Sings.*)

> WE THREE SHOULD NOT BE UNDERESTIMATED –
> WE FIND SUCCESS WHEN UNDER STRESS

DICK BARTON: (*Sings.*)

> MY FRIENDS, I'M SURE TO BE EXONERATED –
> WITH HELP FROM YOU BECAUSE IT'S TRUE!

ALL: (*Sing.*)

> TEAMWORK, TEAMWORK; TEAMWORK SEES YOU THROUGH
> TEAMWORK, TEAMWORK, LOTS OF DERRING-DO
> AND WHEN THE VILLAINS COME TO CALL
> IT'S ALL FOR ONE AND ONE FOR ALL:
> ALL– IN – ALL, THE CALL IS ALL FOR ONE
> AND ONE FOR ALL
> TEAMWORK, TEAMWORK; TEAMWORK SEES YOU THROUGH
> TEAMWORK, TEAMWORK, LOTS OF DERRING-DO
> AND TAKEN ALL – IN – ALL THE CALL IS ALL FOR ONE
> AND ONE FOR ALL

> *KENNY continues alone under the suspended chord, the others eventually notice…*

KENNY: (Sings.)

> AND TAKEN ALL IN ALL
> THE CALL IS ALL FOR ONE
> AND ONE FOR ALL
> AND YOU FOR ME
> AND TWO FOR TEA
> AND TEA FOR TWO
> AND PICTURE ME

JOCK: Kenny, I'm afraid that, what with DB, Snowy and me being back together again, I have no need of a sidekick so, I'm sorry, but I'm going to have to let you go.

KENNY: (*Momentarily crestfallen.*) Och no!… Ah, but…that means that I'm back out there in the market-place, with exciting career moves and fascinating personal challenges just around the corner; a world of exploration

and discovery awaits me! Och, thank you. Thank you.
Ochity Ochity Och. I'm so excited. Thank you, thank
you!

JOCK: Don't mention it.

ALL: (*Sing.*)
SO: ALL IN ALL THE CALL IS ALL FOR ONE
AND ONE FOR ALL!

BBC ANNOUNCER: This must be the most exciting
reunion since the announcement of Bora Minovitch's
Harmonica Rascals Comeback tour of North Cornwall
and the Netherlands. And so our intrepid heroes
endeavour to make their way back to London in time to
intercept Mr Huge's telephone conversation, armed to
the teeth with alliteration and determined to discover the
devilish details of the dangerously dysypygal dastard's
demonic designs.

Scene 12

A street in Soho.

DICK BARTON: Right lads. Here we are. Soho. We must
be on our guard. I happen to know there are ladies of an
unwholesome nature who frequent this particular box.
The most important thing to remember is this. If a lady
approaches you and offers services for money, just
politely refuse. We'd better get in position. I'll stand by
the telephone. One of you can lurk in the shadows,
spoiling for a fight and the other can lean against the
wall with his hat over his eyes, smoking.

JOCK: What sort of services?

DICK BARTON: What?

JOCK: What sort of services? Like a nannying service?

DICK BARTON: No no. I mean like something that's immoral.

SNOWY: You mean like Hercules?

DICK BARTON: No, that's immortal.

SNOWY: So what's the difference then?

DICK BARTON: Between immortal and immoral?

SNOWY: Yeh.

DICK BARTON: One lasts forever and the other's usually over very quickly. Least, that's what my grandfather used to say. And he should know. He was the Bishop of Woolwich.

SNOWY: So what sort of ladies offer these immoral services then?

DICK BARTON: Oh you know, actresses… Doesn't matter. Forget it.

The phone rings.

Ah. It's ringing. Hello?… Do I do what?… No I most certainly do not. And may I suggest that if *you* do, you wash them afterwards and take them to a vet. (*He hangs up.*)

False alarm.

Phone rings again.

Ah! We're in luck! Surely this time.

JOCK: What are you going to do, DB?

DICK BARTON: I'm going to very cleverly find out who Mr Huge's number two is.

JOCK: How?

DICK BARTON: Watch and learn, Jock old boy. Watch and learn. Hello? Number One? This is number two. And my name is?… Sorry?… Well I know I should know it, and of course I do. I was just wondering if you remembered it…well there's no need to… Yes… Yes… Yes… I see. What did you just say?… That's what I thought. (*He hangs up again.*)

Well lads. Looks like we were right. The plot's happening tomorrow night. I'll have to go in disguise.

JOCK: So who is it? Who's number two?

DICK BARTON: Mr Huge.

JOCK/SNOWY: (*Together.*) What?!!!

DICK BARTON: I said Mr Huge.

JOCK/SNOWY: Yes we heard you. We were just expressing surprise with an underlying hint of incredulity.

DICK BARTON: Understood. So Huge is the number two. I knew it. I always thought there was something about him that smelled of number two.

JOCK: So who's number one?

DICK BARTON: I wish I knew. There was something rather familiar about the voice though. We'd better not discuss too much out here. People could be listening. The only clue I can give you is that I have to go, disguised as Mr Huge, to meet this person tomorrow in a famous place named after the Prince Consort, where people get together and sing traditional Empire songs.

SNOWY: Oh no, you don't wanna go there. I go down there all the time. It's 'orrible. Loads of sweaty louts and loose women all jammed in together, drunk as skunks, singin' so loud they spoil the music of the band.

DICK BARTON: I think perhaps we're talking about two different establishments. To which were you referring?

SNOWY: The Royal Albert Hall.

DICK BARTON: Ah. So. Let's meet in the wings of the Albert Hall tomorrow night.

JOCK: Och I'm so excited I cannae wait.

DICK BARTON: Me neither. I wish it was tomorrow night already.

BBC ANNOUNCER: And so Barton's third wish, granted by his friend the Angel, comes true, and tomorrow duly comes. To quote the Bard's darkest play, Tomorrow and tomorrow and tomorrow, I loves ya tomorrow and tomorrow and tomorrow. Unbeknownst to our hero, his supposedly bedridden housekeeper is up and about. Where can she be going? If I'm not very much mistaken, she seems to be preparing for some sort of clandestine rendezvous. Unaware of this mysterious movement, our hero and his two worthy companions find themselves in the wings of the Royal Albert Hall.

Scene 13

The Royal Albert Hall. — Orchestra warm up.

DICK BARTON: Marvellous. Right. How do I look? Do I look convincing?

JOCK: As what?

DICK BARTON: Mr Huge.

JOCK: What does Mr Huge look like?

DICK BARTON: Like this.

JOCK: Then it's very convincing.

DICK BARTON: Thanks Jock. Snowy?

SNOWY: I would never have recognised you.

DICK BARTON: Good man.

SNOWY: Mind you, I wouldn't have recognised him either seeing as how I've never set eyes on him.

DICK BARTON: Quite. Here's the plan. Jock, you wait by the Stage Door just in case the real Mr Huge turns up. If he does, arrest him. Snowy, I want you to go to the BBC.

SNOWY: Why?

DICK BARTON: It's a bit of a gamble, Snowy but I've got a hunch.

SNOWY looks at his back.

Not that sort of hunch, Snowy. Jock, Snowy.

JOCK/SNOWY: (*Together.*) DB. (*They exit.*)

DICK BARTON: Hello?… Hello, number one. This is number two. Are you there, number one?… I repeat, this is number two. Are you there, number one?

BBC ANNOUNCER: (*Emerging from the shadows.*) I'm here, number two.

DICK BARTON: Good God. You!

BBC ANNOUNCER: Of course me. Who were you expecting, the Bridlington girls' choir? Hands up, Barton. I've got a gun.

He begins tying him up through this.

DICK BARTON: So. BBC Announcer. I'm terribly sorry, I've forgotten your name.

BBC ANNOUNCER: Don't worry. So have I. I've been known as BBC Announcer for so long I've completely forgotten the name that my mother gave me.

DICK BARTON: Why don't you ask her?

BBC ANNOUNCER: I have. She doesn't know. She calls me that bloke off the wireless. Not for long though. Soon I will take on my new name and everybody will know who I am. Everywhere I go people will say 'look! There goes Eric Blair!' Tonight, Mr Barton, is just the beginning for me. You see, Barton, what you don't realise is that I have controlled your every move since you went to prison.

DICK BARTON: You framed me?

BBC ANNOUNCER: With a little help. Did you know I have been gradually infiltrating the BBC with my men for a long time now? It was my scriptwriters, editors and studio managers that determined what happened to you. And you didn't even notice.

DICK BARTON: What's the point of all this? Get to the point!

BBC ANNOUNCER: Very well. For some time now, I have been implanting hypnotic suggestions over the wireless, using the frequencies of the pips to induce a pre-hypnotic state in those who hear them. The very last chord of Rule Britannia, which will be sung tonight, contains a note on the organ which will produce the final frequency in the hypnotic code. The public is now neatly primed to receive this signal which will cause them to become mindless automatons, worshipping the BBC as the voice of God. Even you, Dick Barton, will fall prey to my plan being an avid listener of the pips yourself.

DICK BARTON: Yes I have to admit I do like the pips. They keep you regular. So this hypnosis business. What's all that in aid of? I mean what's the point?

BBC ANNOUNCER: As the last piece of the coded jigsaw is played over the airwaves, the King himself will be presented with a declaration giving royal assent to a bill which I myself have drafted, appointing me as Director General and giving the BBC unlimited power over the government.

DICK BARTON: He'll never sign that!

BBC ANNOUNCER: Oh I think he will. He'll have no choice, and he won't even know he's doing it. So what do you think of my plan? Ingenious isn't it? Director General of the BBC! Imagine what I could do in that role. And this is the ingenious bit...

DICK BARTON: I thought that was the ingenious bit.

BBC ANNOUNCER: No that was the clever bit. This is the ingenious bit. I'd control the media. I'd have control of people's minds, the way they think, the way they talk. I'll make them so paranoid they will listen to anything I choose. People will gather round their wireless sets at ungodly hours, transfixed by the sound of other zombies like themselves discussing the clipping of their toenails and trying to work out how to boil cheese. The airwaves will be swamped with that most expendable of commodities... 'real people' – lifeless peasants airing their filthy laundry in front of their unwashed compatriots, egged on by cheap and talentless ex-news readers masquerading as psychotherapists! People will no longer recognise the line between fact and fiction. It'll be like holding up a giant mirror and saying, 'look at this. This is you. See how stupid you are.'

DICK BARTON: There's only one thing wrong with your plan.

BBC ANNOUNCER: What?

DICK BARTON: The British public aren't as gullible as you think, y'know.

BBC ANNOUNCER: Yes they are. In fact I'm probably *over*estimating them. I could make them listen to anything I want. 'It's showtime, ladies and gentlemen! Here you are. I've been up and down the length of the country to find the meaning of your lives and here it is. This tuneless pimply youth is going to sing for you. He's the new Pet Clarke' And you know what? They'd fall over themselves to buy the records. I could probably even put the auditions on a prime time slot and they'd still listen in.

DICK BARTON: I see. Yes, that is a problem. So. Remind me again of your evil motive behind this crazed criminal masterpiece?

BBC ANNOUNCER: I was popular at School. Prefect, I was. Head of the chess club. Opening batsman. And I loved her so much.

DICK BARTON: Who?

BBC ANNOUNCER: Dorabella.

DICK BARTON: Dorabella?

BBC ANNOUNCER: The vicar's daughter. Belladonna I used to call her, before I realised that was the name for poison ivy. She promised to marry me when my voice broke. Then she went to Cambridge to do a degree in applied chemistry.

DICK BARTON: Oh. That Dorabella.

BBC ANN: And she met you, Barton. Good at everything. Captain of everything. Suddenly I was nothing. She fell in love with you, but you weren't interested. It broke her heart. And she broke mine. I never heard from her again.

DICK BARTON: I'm very sorry old chap. But what's all this got to do with your plan?

BBC ANNOUNCER: I've got talent, I have! Gifts! Now. I will rise from the sinking bonfire of mediocrity like a supersonic jet-powered Phoenix on an electric elevator of fire! I've already destroyed you, Barton, and tonight she will see me become the most powerful man in the world, and she'll come running back to me, running, I tell you! She'll beg me to take her back. Oh, Dorabella! If only you could hear me now!

(*Sings.*) WHEN I WAS A BOY...

DICK BARTON: Hadn't you better be going?.

BBC ANNOUNCER: Yes I suppose you're right.

'Rule Britannia' begins in the background.

Yes! Yes! I must go. Goodbye Barton. This is the last time you will recognise me. For when I return, you will be a mindless zombie. Enjoy!

He exits.

DICK BARTON: Dash and blast!

He tries to struggle free. From above, with the aid of a rope, enter CHARLES. — Sir, sir Tarzan

DICK BARTON: Who the...what the...why the...!?

CHARLES: Don't worry sir, all is not lost! I heard every word of the plan. I'm here to save you!

DICK BARTON: Are you mad?! Go away!

CHARLES: What?

DICK BARTON: It's too dangerous for you here. (*CHARLES has untied him by now.*) Wait! What's that blueprint on the floor?

CHARLES: It looks like a blueprint! And someone's dropped it!

Play her as Margaret Thatcher

DICK BARTON: Pick it up, Charles! Yes! I was right. It's the hypnotic code.

CHARLES: And I think I can work it out!

DICK BARTON: Really?

CHARLES: I understand chemical formulae. It's very similar to that. It's easy. Now. I can read the formula but I don't know about music. If only we knew which note was the final frequency in the code.

DICK BARTON: Let's have a look…hmm. F sharp.

CHARLES: Do you know where F sharp is?

DICK BARTON: I do, actually.

CHARLES: Do you?

DICK BARTON: Oh yes.

CHARLES: I didn't know you knew about music. *—Very feminine*

DICK BARTON: You never asked.

CHARLES: Now all we need to do is work out the angles we need to jam the correct F sharp, which we'll do using this… (*Dudley the deadly duck.*) I kept it. It's exactly the right size, shape and weight to jam an organ pipe. Which one's F sharp?

DICK BARTON: That one.

CHARLES: Fantastic!

DICK BARTON: I'm well ahead of your plan, Charles.

CHARLES: I never doubted it for a second.

DICK BARTON: All we need to do is throw it so that it hits the conductor on the back of his head.

CHARLES: Yes! If we get the angle right, the duck will fly directly upwards, while the conductor's toupee falls into the lap of the lead violinist...

DICK BARTON: Exactly...causing her to sneeze her false teeth into the third tuba player's tuba just as he's about to blow...

CHARLES: I see...sending them upwards with such accumulative force that they ricochet against the chandelier onto the duck, who by that time will be at full height...

DICK BARTON: ...causing it to canon into the pipe...

CHARLES: ...jamming the F sharp...

BARTON / CHARLES: (*Together.*) ...just in time to stop the note from being played! I think we make rather a good team, don't you?

CHARLES: Certainly do.

DICK BARTON: Here goes! Alright you fiends, prepare to be out for a duck!

He bowls the duck into the wings, causing a sound effects montage of the above plan. It works.

DICK BARTON and CHARLES celebrate, dancing around. Enter BBC ANNOUNCER.

BBC ANNOUNCER: Who threw that duck? Barton! I might have known. And who the devil are...

CHARLES removes his hat and loosens his hair, revealing himself to be...

BARTON / ANNOUNCER: (*Together.*) Dorabella!!!

BBC ANNOUNCER: (*Sings.*) DORABELLA...

DICK BARTON: Do you mind, that's my song!

DORABELLA: Our song, darling.

BBC ANNOUNCER: But it cannot be.

DORABELLA: It can be, and it does…be.

BBC ANNOUNCER: Dorabella. It's you! And you're with…

DORABELLA: Yes I am. And I love him! I always have and I always will.

BBC ANNOUNCER: That's it. This is more than I can bear… You do realise what this means, don't you? I'm going to have to kill you both.

DORABELLA: (*Throwing herself on DICK BARTON.*) We don't care, do we darling?

DICK BARTON: Certainly not!… Well, perhaps we do a little.

BBC ANNOUNCER: It's no use! The game's over for all of us! I'm going to kill you both, and then I'm going to kill myself.

DICK BARTON: Would you mind awfully doing it the other way round? It's just that…

BBC ANNOUNCER: Silence! I've no more time to waste. It's over, Barton. Say your prayers, I'll see you both in the BBC Canteen! (*He slowly points the gun at them both.*) *She got a gun*

DORABELLA: Oh no! How are we going to get out of this one?

DICK BARTON: There's only one way to find out.

DORABELLA: What's that?

DICK BARTON: I said there's only one w…oh, I see what you mean. I can only pray that Snowy has done his job. Close your ears, Dorabella!

BBC ANNOUNCER: Goodbye Barton! *This bullet puts an end to you...*

DICK BARTON: Snowy! Now!

BBC ANN fires the gun. Instead of shots it plays a recording of 'When I'm Cleaning Windows'.

BBC ANNOUNCER: No!!!

Enter JOCK to arrest him.

DICK BARTON: Well done, Snowy! You can stop now!

It continues.

So. BBC Announcer, that's foiled your little… I said you can stop now!… So. That's foi… Snowy!

It stops.

Thank you.

SNOWY enters very quickly, out of breath.

So that's foiled your little…

SNOWY: DB!

DICK BARTON: Oh, forget it. *– Take her away, Jock.*

BBC ANNOUNCER: It's alright. I've nothing further to say anyway.

JOCK takes him off.

SNOWY: Did I do alright?

DORABELLA: How did you get here so quickly from Broadcasting House?

DICK BARTON: Best not to dwell on the vagaries of BBC Continuity, darling.

JOCK: (*Coming back.*) Darling?

DICK BARTON: Yes. Ladies and gentlemen, since we're all here, I have a little announcement to make.

JOCK: Sorry sir. So do I.

SNOWY: Me too.

DICK BARTON: Alright. Jock. You first.

JOCK: I've just received a telephone call from Mrs Horrocks to say that she's finally been persuaded by her mysterious friend to go abroad to Bavaria where she is going to take the waters and hopefully find a cure. But there's been some trouble with her passport and she's being held by Interpol in a small town called Obergasthausverbotenworst. She wants to know can you go over there and sort it out.

DICK BARTON: I'll get on to it straight away. Sorry darling. Back soon. Snowy?

SNOWY: I've sent the BBC Announcer's forged scripts and sound effects plans to Scotland Yard, who in turn have sent them to the Director of Public Prosecutions, who in turn has sent them to the Lord Chamberlain who is even now briefing...

ANN: (*Offstage.*) The King!

All fall to their knees.

KING: Oh please, there's no need to kneel. Well I suppose I am royalty. Mr Barton, you'll be pleased to know I'm prepared to offer you a full pardon for your sterling efforts, and I hereby restore you to your former post, with immediate effect.

DICK BARTON: That's very kind of your majesty, but now that I've finally got the girl, there are more pressing matters to hand. After I've sorted out Mrs Horrocks' little foreign skirmish, I'm going to retire into family life.

KING: Well I'm speaking purely for myself when I say this, but that sounds fair to us. However, before you go, there is one last thing you can do. It's a very important job, filling a national gaping hole left by tonight's proceedings.

DICK BARTON: You want me to conduct *Land of Hope and Glory?*

KING: Nothing as exciting we're afraid. It's rather a simple job but it is rather pressing. By one's reckoning you'll need to leave in about two minutes ago. There's a car outside for you. One's equerry will fill you in on the way.

DICK BARTON: I'm sure he will. Goodbye darling. Until the next time. Jock. Snowy. Your Majesty.

ALL: DB.

DICK BARTON exits.

KING: Well, ladies and gentlemen. Now that he's gone there's nothing left for me to do but to confer on you a small token of our appreciation. For you, Jock Anderson, the Order of the Trampled Thistle.

JOCK: Och, I'm honoured.

KING: And now. Mr White. Now that I have conferred this token on your esteemed colleague there's nothing left for me to do…so I'll be off.

SNOWY looks a bit miffed.

Enter MRS HORROCKS.

ALL: Mrs Horrocks!

MRS HORROCKS: Before you go, would anybody like a nice cup of hot cocoa?

KING: Oh yes, that would be lovely.

JOCK: Wait a minute! Mrs Horrocks is abroad!

SNOWY: But if Mrs Horrocks is abroad, who the Dickens is…?

MRS HORROCKS pulls a gun out of her handbag and points it at the KING.

DORABELLA: Oh no! How do we get out of this one?

KING: In one's experience, there is usually very little more than one way to find out.

ALL: What's that?

KING: I said there's only one way to find out.

ALL: Yes we heard you, what is it?

DICK BARTON: (*In announcer's booth, looking pissed off.*) Tune in to the next exciting instalment of Dick Barton, Special Agent!

Music: 'The Devil's Gallop'.

The End.

Charlie Nicks -